Bleak House

Charles Dickens

T0345465

Level 4

Retold by Nancy Taylor

Series Editors: Andy Hopkins and Jocelyn Potter

Pearson Education Limited

Edinburgh Gate, Harlow,
Essex CM20 2JE, England
and Associated Companies throughout the world.

ISBN: 978-1-4082-3118-0

This edition first published by Pearson Education Ltd 2010

9 10 8

Text copyright © Pearson Education Ltd 2010

Illustrations by Nick Hardcastle

The moral rights of the authors have been asserted in accordance with
the Copyright Designs and Patents Act 1988

Set in 11/13pt A. Garamond
Printed in China
SWTC/08

Acknowledgements

The publisher would like to thank the following for their kind permission to
reproduce their photographs:

SuperStock: 91

All other images © Pearson Education

Picture research by Frances Topp

Published by Pearson Education Ltd

For a complete list of the titles available in the Pearson English Active Readers series, visit
www.pearsonenglishactivereaders.com.
Alternatively, write to your local Pearson Education office or to
Pearson English Readers Marketing Department, Pearson Education, Edinburgh Gate, Harlow,
Essex CM20 2JE, England.

Contents

1.1 What's the book about?

1 *Bleak House* was written in 1853. Which of the
following subjects would you expect to read
about in a nineteenth-century story? Tick (✓)
your answers.

a ☐ the pleasure of controlling the lives of
other people

b ☐ the high cost of taking problems to a law
court

c ☐ the importance of social class and money

d ☐ the problem of falling in love with the
wrong person

e ☐ the value of giving money to people in
poor countries

f ☐ the difficulty of finding the right profession

g ☐ unhappiness caused by living with terrible
secrets

h ☐ the effects of growing up without parents

2 Discuss the reasons for your answers with other students.

1.2 What happens first?

1 Read the titles of Chapters 1 and 2 on pages 1 and 6, and the words in *italics*
below them. Which of the subjects in 1.1 above do you think you are going
to read about?

2 Discuss these relationships. What are the responsibilities of the people
listed first? How should they help the people listed second? How might the
relationships between them go wrong? Find unfamiliar words in the notes
at the bottom of pages 1–9.

a guardian and ward

b godmother and goddaughter

c rich man and heirs

d lawyer and client

e homeowner and tenant

CHAPTER 1

Life in the Court of Chancery

Wise men say, 'Whatever harm is done to you, do not think of coming here!'
But isn't this a court of justice?

LONDON. A cold, grey November day with thick fog and mud everywhere. Smoke from the dark chimneys produces a soft black rain and the sun hides somewhere in the fog. Dogs, horses, men and women – everything and everyone is lost in the fog.

The **bleak** afternoon is bleakest, and the thick fog is thickest, and the muddy streets are muddiest near the Court of Chancery*. This is often described as the most dangerous, the most **destructive**, the most awful place in heaven or on earth. Wise men say, 'Whatever harm is done to you, do not think of coming here!'

But isn't this a court of **justice**? Yes, but justice is rarely found here and never quickly. The Lord High Chancellor* sits above the noisy crowd and stares out of the window, seeing only fog. The **lawyers** arrive with their endless arguments. A crowd of **suitors** comes every day, waiting for a judgement in their **cases**, which continue for another day, another month, another year. The lawyers grow rich; the suitors die and leave their troubles for their children and grandchildren. Be warned: Chancery destroys lives!

On this typically dull, bleak afternoon, the Court is listening to the most recent arguments in Jarndyce and Jarndyce, the most famous case in Chancery. There is more than one **will**, but which is the legal one? Who is the true **heir** to the Jarndyce fortune? The court has not been able to decide, and the lawyers continue to find more and more points to argue about. The fortune grows

---

* Court of Chancery: a court in which a judge was, in the past, supposed to make fair decisions about property
* Lord High Chancellor: the highest official in the Court of Chancery

bleak /bliːk/ (adj) cold and unpleasant; bad and unlikely to improve
destructive /dɪˈstrʌktɪv/ (adj) damaging people or things so badly that they cannot be repaired
justice /ˈdʒʌstɪs/ (n) the method by which people are judged in courts of law and criminals are punished
lawyer /ˈlɔːjə/ (n) someone whose job is to advise people about the law and speak for them in court
suitor /ˈsuːtə, ˈsjuːtə/ (n) a person who is waiting for a judgement in a legal question. This legal problem is a *suit*.
case /keɪs/ (n) a problem that must be decided in a court of law
will /wɪl/ (n) a legal document in which you say who you want to give your money and property to after you die
heir /eə/ (n) someone who can legally receive the money, property or title of a person after their death

smaller as the costs continue to climb. The last Lord Chancellor said there would be a decision in Jarndyce and Jarndyce when potatoes rained from the sky – an opinion that amused everyone.

The present Chancellor is bored; he looks out into the fog and speaks to one of the regular lawyers. 'Have you finished your argument, Mr Tangle?'

'No, my lord. There are several more points that need to be made and several more of my brother lawyers who will speak.'

Hearing Tangle's words, eighteen more lawyers stand and wave their papers in the direction of the Lord High Chancellor.

'We will continue in two weeks,' the Chancellor commands sleepily, before leaving the courtroom without a backward look. As usual, nothing has happened in the case of Jarndyce and Jarndyce, but behind the scenes, in the great man's private office, something is going to happen that is connected to this case.

◆

Mr Tulkinghorn, a lawyer who is known across the land, leaves Chancery and goes straight to the London house of Sir Leicester Dedlock, one of his many rich and important **clients**. The lawyer wears old-fashioned knee-length trousers, a long coat and a tall hat – all in a dull, dusty black.

The clothes are like the man himself. He is very formal and not at all friendly, although he is often a guest in stylish London apartments and great country houses. He listens and learns, safely locking information away for future use. He speaks only when there is a professional reason for doing so. His secretive methods work well, and by them he has grown very rich and powerful. His clients would be surprised by the amount of knowledge he has of their lives and by the power he holds over them.

Mr Tulkinghorn is the type of man that Sir Leicester has a good opinion of. He is completely British: honest, rich and traditional. And no one knows more about Britishness than Sir Leicester. He is proud of the fact that his family is as old as the hills; the world might continue without hills, but would break down completely without Dedlocks. Mr Tulkinghorn understands Sir Leicester perfectly, and their professional relationship could not be better.

At the age of sixty-six Sir Leicester is at least twenty years older than his very beautiful, very fashionable wife, Lady Honoria Dedlock, but he is energetic in body and mind. In addition to keeping a watchful eye on conditions around the country and knowing which politicians to believe, Sir Leicester, more than anything else, loves his home and his wife. In fact, unlike many men of his class, he married for love, and his love for his wife has never decreased, although she did not bring money or position to her marriage, and she and her husband have no children.

client /ˈklaɪənt/ (n) someone who pays a person or organisation for services or advice

My Lady finds most people and places painfully boring as she moves between the Dedlock country house and London or Paris, searching for something to make her days brighter. She is often sad, but she never speaks of her feelings. She is a good wife, and the public agrees with her husband's very high opinion of her character.

Tulkinghorn is among the many people who greatly admire Lady Dedlock, but he wisely keeps a polite distance between himself and the great lady. On this occasion, though, as on many others, he has a professional reason to speak to her about Jarndyce and Jarndyce. Lady Dedlock has some interest in the case and could receive a small piece of property if it is decided soon.

'My Lady's argument has been heard by the Chancellor again, has it, Mr Tulkinghorn?' asks Sir Leicester as he shakes his lawyer's hand.

'Yes, although as usual nothing important has been done. But because you are leaving soon for Paris, I have brought the most recent papers connected to the case,' says Mr Tulkinghorn, placing some legal documents on a table near Lady Dedlock.

My Lady moves away from the hot fire and looks down at the papers. One sheet catches her attention, and she takes a second look.

'Who copied that piece?' she asks, not stopping to think.

Mr Tulkinghorn, surprised by Lady Dedlock's sudden interest, replies, 'Someone from Mr Snagsby's shop. Why do you ask?'

'No reason. It is so boring, isn't it?' She has turned away from the table, not wanting to appear interested in the document. But then she suddenly turns pale and says, 'I'm afraid I'm not well. The heat ... don't speak to me ... I must go to my room.'

◆

Back in London, the great judge greets three young people who are waiting in his private rooms. The first is a nineteen-year-old man with a handsome, friendly face. The second is his cousin, although they are not close relatives and only met an hour ago. She is an innocent, beautiful girl of seventeen with rich golden hair and soft blue eyes. The third young person is also a stranger to the other two and is not a relative. She is twenty years old and noticeable for her look of kindness and intelligence.

Mr Kenge, a lawyer acting for Mr John Jarndyce of Hertfordshire, introduces the three young people to the Lord High Chancellor. They are Mr Richard Carstone, Miss Ada Clare – both suitors in the case of Jarndyce and Jarndyce – and Miss Esther Summerson.

'What business have they for me?' asks the great judge.

'Mr John Jarndyce, the third living suitor in Jarndyce and Jarndyce, is a cousin of the first two **orphans**, Mr Carstone and Miss Clare. He intends to take care of them and requests that they come to live with him at Bleak House, near the town of St Albans.'

'Is Mr Jarndyce married?' asks the judge.

'He is not, my lord,' says Mr Kenge, 'but Mr Jarndyce has financially supported Miss Summerson, another orphan but not a member of the family, for the last six years. She will share Miss Ada's and Mr Richard's life at Bleak House now that she has completed her studies at Greenleaf School.'

'Very well! Mr John Jarndyce of Bleak House has chosen, it seems, a very good friend for Miss Ada Clare,' the Chancellor begins, looking at Esther. 'And the other arrangements at Bleak House appear to be suitable for these three orphans. Mr Kenge, I leave them in your care.'

Although they only met a few hours earlier in the offices of Kenge and Carboy, Richard, Ada and Esther leave the Court of Chancery like three happy children on a big adventure. Mr Jarndyce's plans for them are still a little mysterious, but they liked each other immediately and now feel very hopeful about starting their new life at Bleak House together.

'Oh! The young **wards** in Jarndyce! Very happy, I am sure, to meet you! It is a good sign when hope and beauty come together in this place,' says an old woman as she steps in front of the little group.

This is Miss Flite. Perhaps she was a suitor in a case in Chancery a long time ago, perhaps not, but now she goes to the court every day and follows the arguments in Jarndyce and Jarndyce very closely.

'Mad!' whispers Richard.

'Right, young man,' replies Miss Flite, who has heard his words. 'I was a

---

orphan /ˈɔːfən/ (n) a child whose parents are dead
ward /wɔːd/ (n) a young person (usually under the age of 21) who is placed under the legal protection of a court or of a responsible adult

young ward myself and not mad at that time. I had hope and, I believe, beauty, but they did not save me. Please accept my good wishes for a judgement in your case.'

'We will leave that to the court, Miss Flite,' Mr Kenge answers politely. 'But now my assistant, Mr Guppy, will take them to Mrs Jellyby's for the night.'

'Who is Mrs Jellyby?' Richard asks, as the three orphans follow Mr Guppy through the narrow streets.

'She is well known for the work she does for poor people, especially in Borrioboola-Gha. I believe that Mr Jarndyce, who is interested in helping the poor and needy, has a high opinion of her good work.' Then, walking beside Miss Summerson, Mr Guppy continues, 'Quite a foggy day, isn't it, miss?' He seems to be taking a special interest in the young lady.

'The fog is certainly very thick!' Esther replies.

'But it has no harmful effect on you, miss,' Mr Guppy continues politely. 'In fact, it seems to do you good, miss, if I can judge by your appearance.'

CHAPTER 2

Esther's Story: A Home at Last

'Esther, you have new friends, a new house and new duties. It is time to forget about your past difficulties. You are going to be happy here.'

It is very difficult to write my part of this story, because I know I am not clever. I grew up in a cold, lonely house, looked after by Miss Barbary, my **godmother**. Although she was clearly a good, religious woman who did her duty towards me, she was not able to show me any love or warmth.

My godmother sent me to school but kept me separate from the other girls; in fact, I never went out for any social occasions. My birthday was never celebrated and was only spoken about one terrible time. We were sitting silently near the fire, when suddenly my godmother said, 'Little Esther, your birthday is the saddest day of the year.'

I began to cry and said, 'Oh, dear godmother, tell me, please, did my mother die on my birthday? Please tell me about her.'

My godmother looked at me coldly and finally said, 'Your mother is your **disgrace**, and you were hers. Your life will always have a shadow over it. You must work hard, obey me and stay in the background.'

That night I felt more alone than ever, but I promised myself I would be strong and try to do some good to someone. Perhaps one day, if I were kind and cheerful, I could win some love for myself.

Our lives continued in this sad, quiet way for another two years until I was almost fourteen. One evening, when I was reading to my godmother, a terrible noise came from her throat and she fell to the floor. She never opened her eyes again.

After my godmother's body was in the ground, Mr Kenge, a lawyer from Kenge and Carboy in London, appeared at the house.

'Miss Summerson,' he began, 'your late aunt left you nothing, but ...'

'My aunt, sir!'

'Yes, Miss Barbary was your aunt, and she received an offer of help two years ago from Mr John Jarndyce. Your aunt refused the kind, unselfish offer, but Mr Jarndyce is now offering it again. You will go to a school for young ladies. Your only responsibility to Mr Jarndyce is to work hard and prepare yourself for future employment.'

---

godmother /ˈɡraʊl/ (n) a woman who promises at a special religious service to be a child's religious guide
disgrace /dɪsˈɡreɪs/ (n/v) a person or thing that is thought to be very bad and unacceptable; the end of other people's good opinion of you. If you *disgrace* someone, your bad behaviour makes them feel ashamed.

After six wonderful, happy years at Greenleaf School, I received a letter telling me that Mr Jarndyce had a job for me. The pupils and teachers said goodbye with many kisses, many sad tears and many good wishes.

I felt quite nervous in London when I was taken to the offices of Kenge and Carboy. But there I met two people who became my best friends: Ada Clare and Richard Carstone. We were three orphans on our way to a new life at Bleak House, Mr John Jarndyce's home.

After meeting with the Lord High Chancellor, we were taken by Mr Guppy, the young lawyer from the office of Kenge and Carboy, to Mrs Jellyby's house. There we followed Mr Guppy up a dark flight of stairs, falling over children and rubbish as we went, finally finding Mrs Jellyby. Like her children, the lady herself was not only untidy but also quite dirty.

'Oh, it's the guests!' cried Mrs Jellyby when she looked up at last. 'You must excuse me – my work for our poor sisters and brothers in Borrioboola-Gha is so important.'

After a disorderly meal of fish, meat and potatoes that were not quite cooked, Mrs Jellyby continued her work for Africa, forgetting about us and her children. When it was nearly midnight, Ada and I went upstairs.

'I am surprised that Mr Jarndyce sent us here!' said Ada.

'It *must* be very good of Mrs Jellyby to work so hard for the poor people in Borrioboola-Gha,' I agreed, 'but look at the children and this dirty, disorganised house!'

'I think *you* could change this house into a home in no time,' Ada said. She was the sweetest, gentlest girl I had ever met, and I already loved her dearly.

In the morning, during a walk, we three orphans met the old lady from the day before.

'Good morning! Very happy to see you, I am sure!' cried Miss Flite. 'May I invite you to my little apartment? A visit from the wards of Jarndyce would give me great pleasure.'

Miss Flite led us to a strange shop with this sign above the door: KROOK: **RAG** AND BOTTLE MARKET. A second sign said that Mr Krook would buy anything: bones, cooking pots, old iron, waste paper, men's and ladies' clothes, bottles, books, human hair. There were piles of papers inside which reminded me of my letters from Kenge and Carboy, written in what is called 'law-hand*'. Then I saw another notice on the wall in this same style of writing: a gentleman named Nemo wanted employment in copying legal documents. He could be contacted at Mr Krook's shop.

'Mr Krook,' Miss Flite said to the shop owner. 'Here is a surprise for you. My young friends are suitors in Jarndyce and Jarndyce.'

'Well, well,' the strange old man said, 'I wish you better luck than old Tom Jarndyce. He spent many hours in this shop, but he came to an awful end.'

'That's enough, Krook,' said Miss Flite. 'Do not frighten them.'

Later, as we left her apartment above the shop, Miss Flite pointed to the door of Mr Nemo's room. 'Krook's other **tenant**,' she whispered.

'Ah, cousin, I think this Chancery is a hard place,' said Richard when we

---

* law-hand: a special type of handwriting used by a law-writer for legal documents

rag /ræg/ (n) a piece of old cloth or old clothing

tenant /'tenənt/ (n) someone who lives in a house or room and pays rent to the person who owns it

were outside in the street.

'Yes,' agreed Ada. 'Why can't the court come to a judgement in our case?'

'It is a mystery, I agree. But whatever happens, Ada, Chancery will work none of its awful power on *us*. We have been brought together, thanks to our good cousin Jarndyce, and the Court can't separate us now!'

'Never, I hope, cousin Richard!' said Ada gently.

I could see that Richard shared my high opinion of Ada. She was a beautiful young girl and her character matched her beauty.

Soon we began the next stage of our journey to Bleak House. The three of us were quite nervous and excited by the time we reached St Albans and saw the lights of an old-fashioned house at the end of a long driveway. The front door opened and Mr John Jarndyce appeared, standing in a stream of light.

'Ada, my love, Esther, my dear, welcome to your home! I am very happy to see you! Rick, let me shake your hand. Please come in!'

In the sitting-room, I had an opportunity to examine our **guardian** as he asked us about our journey. He had a handsome, energetic face which was always changing, and his hair was silvery grey. I guessed that he was about sixty years old, but he was still strong and full of energy.

Later, as I was putting my clothes away, I heard a soft knock on my door.

'For you, miss,' said a young servant as she handed me a basket of keys.

I gave my basket of housekeeping keys a shake and said to myself, 'Esther, you have new friends, a new house and new duties. It is time to forget about your past difficulties. You are going to be happy here.'

◆

After breakfast on my first morning at Bleak House, Mr Jarndyce called me into a small room which seemed to be part library and part office.

'Sit down, my dear,' said Mr Jarndyce. 'This, you need to know, is a special place. I call it the **Growlery** because it is where I come to growl and complain, and I spend quite a lot of time in here.

'You know, Esther, you have earned my high opinion by your hard work and good character, and I hope to continue as your guardian and friend. Now, what do you think about this Chancery business?'

'I have heard that it is about a will, but I am afraid I don't understand why it has been in the court for so long, or how it will come to an end,' I told him.

'The lawyers have taken so many different directions that the will is only about costs now. Most of the Jarndyce fortune has disappeared. My cousins

---

guardian /grɑːdɪən/ (n) someone who is legally responsible for another person's child
growl /grɑʊl/ (v) to complain in a low, angry voice. A *growlery*, in this book, is a place where someone goes when they are feeling bad-tempered.

and I are caught in this mess because we were named as suitors, and we cannot escape from it until the court reaches a decision.

'Old Tom Jarndyce changed the name of this house from The Peaks to Bleak House because our case made him feel so bleak about the future. Fortunately, the house was not in Chancery; other Jarndyce properties were, and they will be sold to pay the costs, but we have Bleak House, and I hope it will be a comfortable and cheerful home for you and Ada and Rick.'

'It seems to be a very friendly place, sir ...' I said.

'I think you had better call me Guardian, my dear,' said Mr Jarndyce.

This kindness touched my heart, and I had to give my keys a little shake to control my emotions.

'I hope, Guardian, that I can help to make the house a happy place.'

'Esther, with your cheerful attitude, we shall have to forget that the Growlery exists. But we must return to business. Rick must have a profession. What can be done for him?'

'Perhaps we should ask Mr Richard about his own preference,' I suggested. I couldn't believe that my guardian was asking for *my* advice!

'Exactly. Little woman, I am sure you will know how to discuss the subject with him. And now, my dear, I think we are finished with the Growlery for today! But do you wish to ask me anything while we are here?'

'About myself, sir? And my background?' I asked.

'Yes. I want your heart and mind to be at rest.'

'Guardian, I am confident that you would tell me if there was anything that I needed to know.' From that moment I decided to stop wondering about my past. In addition, I forgot my girlish dream that Mr Jarndyce was, perhaps, my father.

◆

I soon learned how generous Mr Jarndyce was in many more ways – to people like Mrs Jellyby, who asked for money for their work, and also to his friends and neighbours. One morning he asked Ada and me to visit some poor brick-makers and their families to see if we could help them.

We went to the brick-field and found the house that Mr Jarndyce was worried about, knocked and were let into a cold, dark room. Beside the small fire, there was a woman with a black eye holding a sick-looking baby; a man lay on the floor, smoking a pipe and appearing to our eyes to be drunk.

'Have you come to have tea and cakes?' asked the man. 'Or have you come to tell us that our house is dirty and that we've got no work and no money?'

Ada and I felt that it was rude to interrupt these people's lives. But the man on the floor turned his back to us and seemed to fall asleep, so we went quietly to the woman beside the fire and asked if the baby was ill.

She only looked at the poor little one as it lay in her arms. Ada gently bent down and touched the little face. As she did so, I understood what had happened and gently pulled her back. The child had died.

I took the baby, placed it gently on a shelf and covered it with my own handkerchief. We tried to calm the mother, but her tears did not stop as she stared at her child – the sixth baby, she told us, that she had lost.

◆

One morning as I sat at my desk checking the housekeeping bills, a servant came to tell me that Mr Guppy had arrived and wished to speak to me.

He entered and said, 'Miss, may I have a minute's conversation with you? A private conversation between you and me?'

'I will not discuss your business with anyone, if that is your request.'

'Thank you, miss.' Mr Guppy then dropped to his knees. 'At present I earn two pounds a week at Kenge and Carboy. I have an apartment in one of the healthiest parts of London. Miss Summerson! I admire you. I love you. Would you be kind enough to become my wife?'

I was shocked. 'Mr Guppy, please stand up. I thank you for your honest feelings, but I cannot become your wife,' I answered. 'I do not love you.'

'Cruel miss,' said Mr Guppy, 'from the day I met you, I have carried your sweet face in my heart. If you change your mind, and I hope you will, please contact me at Kenge and Carboy.'

When I was alone, I began to laugh, and then surprised myself by starting to cry. I felt confused and shaken by Mr Guppy's visit. In some way it had reminded me of my past, a time when no one had had any feelings for me.

2.1 Were you right?

Think back to your answers to Activity 1.2 on page iv. Then write the names.

1 Who has no time for her children but works hard for
the people of Borrioboola-Gha? ....

2 Who grew up in a cold, lonely house without love
or kindness? ....

3 Who values people who have a similarly high
position in society as he and his family? ....

4 Who needs to start thinking about getting a job? ....

5 Who lost hope and beauty because of the legal system? ....

6 Who asks someone to share his future but is refused? ....

7 Who succeeds in life by controlling other people? ....

8 Who behaves differently from usual after being
reminded of the past? ....

2.2 What more did you learn?

Circle the right words in *italics*.

1 The area around the Court of Chancery gives people *hope / without hope*.

2 The *suitors / lawyers* are the people who usually collect the most money from a
case in Chancery.

3 Mr Tulkinghorn aims to keep his business as *hidden / open* as possible.

4 Sir Leicester Dedlock married for *love / money and social position*.

5 John Jarndyce is a cousin of *Esther / Richard and Ada*.

6 Miss Barbary *was / was not* Esther Summerson's close blood relative.

7 Ada and Esther *criticise / admire* Mrs Jellyby's housekeeping skills.

8 Mr Nemo and Miss Flite both *work for / rent a room from* Mr Krook.

9 Mr Jarndyce's actions show his *generous / selfish* character.

10 The brick-makers near Bleak House have *an easy / a hard* life.

2.3 Language in use

Look at the sentences on the right. Then complete the sentences below with a word from the box below and the correct form of the verb in *italics*.

> **After meeting** with the Lord High Chancellor, we were taken to Mrs Jellyby's house.
>
> I surprised myself **by starting** to cry.

after   in addition to   by   in   of   before

1 .... (*travel*) to Bleak House, the orphans sleep in London.

2 Mrs Jellyby is interested .... (*help*) the poor people in Africa.

3 Mr Nemo earns money .... (*copy*) legal documents.

4 Miss Barbary was Esther's guardian .... (*be*) her aunt.

5 .... (*meet*) Esther, Mr Guppy wants her to be his wife.

6 Mr Krook's method .... (*buy*) and .... (*sell*) is unusual.

2.4 What happens next?

Chapter 3 follows the style of Chapter 1; Chapter 4 follows Chapter 2. Write 3 or 4 according to the chapter in which you expect to find these:

1 Verbs in present time   ----

2 Verbs in past time   ----

3 Esther Summerson telling her own story   ----

4 An unnamed story-teller   ----

5 Centres of activity: Mr John Jarndyce's houses   ----

6 Centres of activity: the area around the Court of Chancery and Sir Leicester Dedlock's country house   ----

7 Activity often controlled by Mr Tulkinghorn   ----

8 Activity often managed by Mr John Jarndyce   ----

Documents and Death

'Are you the boy I have read about in the newspapers?'
'I don't know,' says Jo. 'I don't know nothing about nothing.'

The handsome, wonderfully tidy Mrs Rouncewell is the housekeeper at Chesney Wold, Sir Leicester and Lady Dedlock's house in Lincolnshire. As she says, her job is the house and the family, both of which she has looked after very responsibly for more than fifty years.

Most of the rooms at Chesney Wold are shut, because Sir Leicester and Lady Honoria Dedlock are now in Paris. But Mrs Rouncewell has a visitor with her in the kitchen: her grandson, Watt. He is the son of Mrs Rouncewell's elder son, a successful engineer and businessman. Her younger son, George, on the other hand, was a little wild when he was young. He became a soldier and never returned to Chesney Wold. George was a clever, happy boy who was popular with everyone, and was his mother's favourite child. Mrs Rouncewell's grandson did well at school and now has a place in his father's business. Soon he will start his own family. In fact, that may be what he is thinking about now.

'Grandmother,' he says shyly, 'what did you call that girl who was helping you when I arrived? She is very pretty, isn't she?'

'That was Rosa. She is from the village and a very good worker and a clever girl. But listen, do you hear the sound of wheels?'

Rosa returns to report that two young men are in the hall and have requested to see the house. 'They asked me to give you this card.'

Watt reads the card for his grandmother: 'Mr Guppy, lawyer, colleague of Mr Tulkinghorn, London.'

When she hears the name of Sir Leicester's lawyer, Mrs Rouncewell agrees that Rosa can show the house to the men, and Watt happily follows.

Mr Guppy and his friend, Mr Tony Jobling, are soon bored. Is there no end to the beautiful rooms, long hallways, and paintings of long-dead Dedlocks? But when they enter the formal sitting-room, an oil painting over the fireplace wakes Mr Guppy up. He stares at it with uncommon interest.

'Well, well!' the young lawyer says. 'Who is that?'

'The picture,' says Rosa, 'is of the present Lady Dedlock. It is a perfect copy of the lady, and the best work of the painter.'

'You know,' says Mr Guppy to his friend as they leave Chesney Wold, 'I have never seen Lady Dedlock, but I feel certain that I know her!'

◆

Back in London we see Mr Tulkinghorn leaving his old-fashioned rooms, which serve as his home as well as his office. He goes straight to Snagsby's Office Materials, Law-Writing and Copying shop in Cook's Court.

'Mr Tulkinghorn! This is a rare surprise!' cries Mr Snagsby.

'Jarndyce and Jarndyce,' says Mr Tulkinghorn, wasting no time on a greeting and placing a document on Snagsby's desk. 'You copied this for me recently. It is in a law-hand that I admire. Who copied it?'

Mr Snagsby checks his order book and says, 'That went to Nemo, a law-writer who lives above Krook's rag and bottle shop. Very near here.'

'Nemo!' says Mr Tulkinghorn. 'A name that means "no one" in Latin! Can you show me Krook's shop as I leave?'

'Of course, sir, please follow me,' says Mr Snagsby very politely as he opens the shop door. 'The advantage of Mr Nemo is that he will work through the night if the job is urgent. Here we are – Krook's shop.'

'Thank you, Snagsby, you can leave me now.'

Old Krook comes forward with a lamp as the lawyer enters.

'Excuse me,' says the lawyer. 'Is Mr Nemo in?'

'I don't know. Second floor, sir. Take the lamp, and be careful,' advises Krook. 'Mr Nemo is a strange man with dark moods.'

Tulkinghorn knocks on the door of the law-writer's room, receives no answer, opens the door and walks in. He finds a room which is nearly black with smoke and dirt. Beside the chimney there are two old chairs, an old suitcase, and a broken desk with a few sheets of paper and a bottle of ink on it. No carpet on the floor and no curtains at the window.

On the low bed the lawyer can see a man lying half covered under a pile of rags. His face looks yellow and his hair and beard have not been cut for a long time. The air in the room smells strange – and then the lawyer recognises the bitterness of **opium**.

Krook appears at the lawyer's elbow. 'Can't you wake him?'

'No. Does the man generally sleep like this?' whispers Mr Tulkinghorn. He touches the man. 'God save us! He is dead.'

Krook looks at Tulkinghorn and shouts, 'Send for a doctor! Call up the stairs for Miss Flite, sir. Here's poison beside the bed. Quick!'

Mr Tulkinghorn goes into the hall, shouts and sends Miss Flite out for a doctor. This gives Krook, a man who never misses an opportunity, just enough time to examine Nemo's old suitcase, and then return to the dead man's side, before the lawyer is in the room again.

Soon a young doctor rushes up the stairs and after one look says, 'He has

opium /ˈəʊpiəm/ (n) a very strong drug

been dead for about three hours. I recognise him – he has bought opium from me for the last year and a half. There is enough of it in his old teapot to kill ten people or more.' He thinks for a minute or two. 'He probably took too much accidentally, but perhaps it was a happy escape from a hard life. You can see that he used to have a handsome face and a good figure. Maybe too much had gone wrong for him.'

Tulkinghorn watches Krook open the old suitcase, but very little is found: some old clothes, a few old newspapers, an empty envelope that smells of opium – nothing more. The cupboard and drawers are empty.

◆

The next day, a judge calls witnesses to decide how Mr Nemo, aged forty-five, died. Snagsby, Krook, Miss Flite and Tulkinghorn answer questions about the man and his death. Finally a very pale, thin boy in rags is pushed forward by Krook's neighbours.

'Now, young man, what is your name?' asks the judge.

'Jo,' the boy answers. 'Just Jo.'

After hearing that Jo cannot read or write, has no family or friends and exists by earning a few pennies for sweeping the streets, the judge decides that he is not acceptable as a witness and sends him away.

The judge addresses the crowd: 'Accidental death. This case is closed.'

As he leaves, we see Mr Tulkinghorn in the corner of the room interviewing young Jo,

'How did you meet Mr Nemo?' the lawyer asks.

'He saw me one terrible cold winter night. I was trying to get warm in a doorway. When I told him I had no one and nothing, he gave me the price of supper and a night's rent. After that, when he saw me, if he had any money in his pocket, he always gave me something, but some nights he said, "I'm as poor as you today, Jo." He was very good to me, he was!'

Perhaps Jo is not the only person on earth who would be sorry to learn of Mr Nemo's death. In brighter days, there was a fire in him that burned for one woman – and she also held him in her heart. But where is she when his body is placed in the **burial ground** with the poorest of London's dead?

That night, after everyone is in their beds, a small figure returns to Nemo's final resting place. He sweeps the steps outside the locked gates and then looks in. Before he leaves, Jo whispers: 'He was very good to me, he was!'

◆

The rain has finally stopped in Lincolnshire, but even the sun and Mrs Rouncewell's warm greeting do not brighten Lady Dedlock's mood as she and her husband return to Chesney Wold.

Lady Dedlock is surprised to see a new servant and asks Mrs Rouncewell about the girl.

'Rosa is a young student of mine, My Lady. She is nineteen years old.'

Lady Dedlock lightly touches Rosa's shoulder with two fingers. 'Be a sensible girl. You will need more than beauty in this life.'

'Yes, My Lady,' answers Rosa. Her shyness makes her even prettier.

Hortense, a Frenchwoman who has been My Lady's **maid** for five years, has a different opinion of Rosa and her beauty. She makes a nasty joke to the other servants about the attention that Lady Dedlock gives the young girl. They understand that Hortense is horribly jealous; in fact, they know that she can be dangerous, and they keep out of her way.

After dinner on the Dedlocks' first evening at home, a visitor quietly appears in the sitting-room. He wears his usual calm, serious look.

'Tulkinghorn! Any news from town?' asks Sir Leicester.

The lawyer brings Sir Leicester up to date about several pieces of business, and then he turns to Lady Dedlock.

'My Lady, do you remember a piece of law-writing that interested you before your trip to Paris?'

'It sounds slightly familiar.' My Lady is not willing to communicate any interest in the matter to Tulkinghorn.

'I found the writer of that document,' reports Tulkinghorn, while watching

---

burial ground /ˈberiəl ɡraʊnd/ (n) a place where dead bodies are put into the ground, or *buried*

maid /meɪd/ (n) a female servant, especially in a large house

Lady Dedlock closely. 'I found him in a poor, dirty room, dead from taking too much opium, probably by accident.'

'Tell me about him!' says Lady Dedlock. 'What kind of man was he?'

'Very difficult to say,' replies the lawyer, shaking his head. 'He lived in terrible conditions, but the young doctor believed that he had had a better life in the past – that he was probably a gentleman. He used the name of Nemo, which, I am sure you know, means "no one" in Latin.'

'Certainly an interesting story – at least for a minute or two,' says Lady Dedlock as she stares calmly at the lawyer.

Lady Dedlock wants to know how much information the lawyer has about Nemo. He wants to know why she is interested in the dead man. Neither asks. For very different reasons they both keep their secrets locked safely in their own hearts.

◆

Lady Dedlock seems anxious and cannot stay in one place – this morning she was at Chesney Wold; tomorrow she may be abroad. Even her husband cannot understand her reasons for moving from place to place so often.

In the evening of this day, a woman passes unnoticed under the windows of Mr Tulkinghorn's house in London. If you look closely, you will see that she is dressed as a servant – clearly one of the more important ones from a good house – but she looks and moves like a lady. She is wearing a long dark coat and a **veil** over her face; she never turns her head to the left or right until she comes to the crossroads where poor Jo is sweeping the mud from the streets. She goes near him and whispers, 'Follow me.'

When they are in a quiet corner the lady behind the veil asks, 'Are you the boy I have read about in the newspapers?'

'I don't know,' says Jo. 'I don't know nothing about nothing.'

'Are you the boy who answered a judge's questions about Mr Nemo?'

'Yes, that's me!'

'Speak in a whisper! Now, tell me, was Mr Nemo very ill and poor when he was alive? Did he look as bad as you?' asks the woman, feeling sick at the thought because Jo looks more like a hungry animal than a boy.

'Oh, not as bad as me,' says Jo. 'Did you know him, My Lady?'

'I am not a lady. I am a servant. Can you show me where Mr Nemo lived and worked, where he died, where they took his body?'

'I know all of that,' whispers Jo.

'Go in front of me and show me these terrible places. Stop at each, but do not speak and do not look at me. Follow my orders, and I will pay you well.'

veil /veɪl/ (n) a thin piece of material that women wear to cover their faces

Jo listens carefully and then leads the woman to Snagsby's shop, then to Krook's Rag and Bottle Market and finally to Nemo's final resting place.

'He was put there,' says Jo, pointing through the bars. 'In the corner, over there among those piles of bones and close to that kitchen window!'

The woman rests against the wall and stays quiet for some minutes. Then she takes off her glove and finds a coin in her purse. Jo notices her small white hand and beautiful rings. She drops a coin into the boy's hand without touching it, and before he looks up she has disappeared.

CHAPTER 4

Esther's Story: A Face and a Voice

Her fashionable appearance and her proud attitude were completely new to me,
but a picture of myself – sad, lonely little Esther – came into my mind.

The discussions about Richard's future profession continued, but unfortunately every suggestion seemed equally attractive to him. One day he decided to go to sea, and the next he was thinking about becoming a lawyer.

'I am worried about Rick's character,' Mr Jarndyce said to me one day in the Growlery. 'He delays making decisions because he is always expecting a result in Jarndyce and Jarndyce. The case is affecting his judgement.'

'I am sure I don't want to go into the Church,' Richard said that afternoon, 'but anything else would suit me.'

'Medicine –' suggested our guardian finally.

'Yes!' shouted Richard enthusiastically. 'I am sure I would like to be a doctor!'

I doubt if he had ever had this thought before, but at that moment Richard was certain that his path was now clear – he would become a doctor.

With Mr Jarndyce's help, Richard agreed to become a student of Mr Bayham Badger, a well-known doctor with a good **practice** in London.

Before Richard left for London, Ada surprised me one evening after a dinner party with a few guests, including one or two doctors, by rushing into my bedroom and whispering, 'My dear Esther! I have a great secret to tell you! My cousin Richard says – I know it is foolish, we are both so young – but he says ... that he loves me with all his heart.'

'Does he really?' said I. 'Dear Ada, I realised that weeks ago!'

'You are so clever! And I love him, too! With my whole heart!' She looked so pretty and so happy that my eyes filled with tears.

The next day, Mr Jarndyce talked to Ada and Richard about their news. 'My dear cousins, you and Esther have made my house bright and happy. From early days, I began to think that you two cousins might decide to go through life together – but it must be a plan for the future.'

'We are in no hurry, sir,' replied Richard.

'That is sensible because you are very young,' continued Mr Jarndyce. 'Things may change, and you may decide that you are happy as cousins and nothing more. If that is your decision, please don't be afraid to talk to me. Your love is strong, but for a successful future you must be serious about your medical studies, Rick, and prepare yourself to be a good husband. And that is enough advice for today! I am very happy for you both!'

practice /ˈpræktɪs/ (n) the work of a doctor or lawyer, or the place where they work

'Sir,' replied Richard again. 'We will always want your advice, and we will always be grateful to you for everything you have given us.'

'Dear cousin John,' said Ada sweetly, 'I give you all the love and duty I could have for a parent.'

I have forgotten to say that one of the guests at our small dinner party the night before was a young doctor, rather shy. Ada asked me later if I thought he was sensible and pleasant, and I said yes.

◆

When the day came for Richard to leave Bleak House, I was especially pleased that he asked me to look after Ada, his future wife. 'And if our suit in Chancery makes us rich – which it may, you know ...'

A shadow crossed Ada's lovely, usually hopeful face.

'My dearest Ada,' continued Richard, 'why not? The longer the case goes on, the closer we come to a decision. Isn't that certain?'

'You know best, Richard. But I'm afraid that if we hope for a decision in Jarndyce and Jarndyce, we will be poor and very unhappy.'

Ada, Mr Jarndyce and I travelled to London with Richard, leaving him at the home of Mr Badger. While we were there, we went to Miss Flite's room and found her with her doctor. After greeting us, the young medical gentleman said, 'Miss Flite is much better and may appear in court tomorrow. She has been greatly missed there, I understand.'

'And a visit from the wards in Jarndyce and Jarndyce of Bleak House – this is a rare pleasure under my simple roof,' said the old lady.

'Have you been very ill?' asked Mr Jarndyce kindly.

'Very unwell! Not pain, you know – trouble. We have had death here – Mr Nemo, the law-writer – and it frightened me. But Mr Woodcourt – you know my doctor, I believe – he is so kind. Krook!?' said Miss Flite suddenly. 'Why are you listening at my door?'

The old man pushed into the

room. 'Your servant, Mr Jarndyce,' he began. 'I knew old Tom Jarndyce well, but I have never seen *you* in Court.'

'I have no wish to go there,' said Mr Jarndyce.

'Maybe you are right, because there will never be a judgement in Jarndyce and Jarndyce, will there?'

At last we escaped from Krook, and in the street Mr Jarndyce asked Mr Woodcourt if the old man was mad.

'No, not yet,' the doctor answered, 'but he drinks a large quantity of alcohol every day, and he has strange ideas.'

I have forgotten to say that Mr Woodcourt was the same young doctor who had joined us at Bleak House for dinner. And did I say that Mr Jarndyce invited him to dinner again after our visit to Miss Flite's?

◆

I was worried about Richard's attitude to his medical studies, but kept my thoughts to myself because Ada was always so enthusiastic about everything connected with her cousin. Unfortunately, I learned that Mr Badger shared my worries when I had a private conversation with him one afternoon at Mr Jarndyce's London apartment.

'Mr Carstone is very well and very good company at the dinner table. If I am honest, though, I wonder if he has chosen his profession wisely. In fact, I believe he is bored by it. Young men like your friend Mr Allan Woodcourt learned to work very hard and to live on very little money during their medical training. I don't think Mr Carstone has the same deep interest in the profession,' Mr Badger explained.

Ada and I had an opportunity to speak to Richard the next evening. After some light conversation, I asked, 'And how is your training going, Richard?'

'Good enough!' he said. 'It will do as well as anything else until our suit is decided. Oh, I forgot, I shouldn't talk about our case in Chancery. If I am honest, medicine doesn't really suit me. But let's forget about it for now.'

'Richard, I am afraid we cannot forget about it,' I said very seriously.

'Dear, dear Esther, you are right. I become quite angry with myself because I love my cousin so much and want her to be proud of me. You know that, don't you, Ada? But I find it so difficult to study every day for long hours. Maybe I went into medicine too quickly, without enough thought,' Richard said quite cheerfully. 'And, do you know, I have actually been thinking that perhaps the law is the profession for me!'

'The law!' repeated Ada, turning pale.

'If I went into Kenge's office,' said Richard, 'I could keep an eye on our suit – I am sorry to talk about it again, but I could study it and look after our interests, and I would work very hard because it would help us, Ada.'

Mr Jarndyce was patient with Richard, and after several long meetings, he agreed to help him get a position at Kenge and Carboy to study law.

One evening, after everything had been arranged and Richard had begun his new studies, Ada spoke quietly to our guardian. 'Cousin John,' she began, 'I hope that your opinion of Richard has not been affected by his change from medicine to law. I don't want you to think badly of him.'

'No, my love,' said Mr Jarndyce. 'I would only think badly of him if his actions ever made you unhappy. Time is on his side, and he can make a success of the law. I promise that my high opinion of Rick has not changed.'

But I must tell you that I noticed that my guardian's look was less hopeful and more troubled as he watched Ada leave the room. This look worried me and I could not sleep that night. At about three o'clock in the morning I was still awake and went quietly downstairs to find my work basket. I was surprised to see a light in the Growlery and knocked gently at the door.

'Esther! What is this? Is there some trouble?' Mr Jarndyce asked.

'No, Guardian. I couldn't sleep, but why are you here? You have no trouble, I hope, to keep you awake?'

'No, little woman, but I hope you will stay and talk to me. I have decided that it is my duty to tell you the few facts that I know about your history.

'Nine years ago I received a very sad letter from your aunt, describing your situation: an orphan girl of twelve whose mother was her disgrace. She told me that she had kept the details of your background a secret and added that when she died, you would be left without friends, family or even a name. She had given you a false name so you would not be connected to her family in any way. Your situation affected me, and now I must say how happy I am every hour of every day that you have come to Bleak House.'

'Dear Guardian, you have become a father to me! I am happier than you!'

At the word 'father', Mr Jarndyce looked shocked and troubled, but the look quickly disappeared and he smiled at me.

'Accept a fatherly good-night, my dear,' he said. 'These are late hours for working and thinking. You do that for all of us all day long, little woman.'

We had a visitor next day – Mr Allan Woodcourt, who by then had been to see us several times. He was going to China and to India to work as a doctor on board a ship. He was going to be away a long, long time. He was not rich, and much of his work was with poor people in London. This trip, I believe, was a way for him to make some money so he could start his own medical practice when he returned.

Before he left our house, Mr Woodcourt said to my guardian, 'Sir, I want to thank you for many happy hours in your home. I will take the memory of them with me and will remember each of you when I am far away.'

Later that day, a servant came into my workroom with a small, pretty bunch of flowers. 'They were left at the door for you, miss, by someone who was hurrying away to join a ship.'

♦

After several months in London, Ada and I went to Lincolnshire with Mr Jarndyce to visit one of his oldest and best friends, Mr Lawrence Boythorn. This big, friendly man met us at the village near his house, and after greeting us warmly, he led our **carriage** and horses to his property.

'I must apologise,' he said before we began, 'but this trip will be about two kilometres longer than it should be. Our straightest road lies through Sir Leicester Dedlock's park, but we have a disagreement about the piece of land between our two properties and so we keep away from each other.'

On Sunday we all walked to the little church in the park for the morning service. Mr Boythorn pointed out a number of people who were servants at Chesney Wold, including the old housekeeper, Mrs Rouncewell, a very pretty young maid named Rosa, and a handsome but cross-looking Frenchwoman called Miss Hortense.

As the bells rang, Sir Leicester and Lady Dedlock entered the church and everyone stood up. I looked at Lady Dedlock. Her eyes met mine and her handsome proud face seemed to come alive for just a moment. My heart was beating quickly. Why did this beautiful face remind me of my godmother? Her fashionable appearance and her proud attitude were completely new to me, but a picture of myself – sad, lonely little Esther – came into my mind. I was shaken by these emotions and these memories, but I calmed myself and looked towards Lady Dedlock again. She was not looking at me and my heart slowed down.

During our visit, Mr Jarndyce, Ada and I enjoyed many long walks in the countryside

carriage/ˈkærɪdʒ/ (n) a vehicle with wheels that is pulled by a horse or horses

near Mr Boythorn's house and found several favourite spots. One Saturday, we were sitting under a tree on a lovely hill when we heard thunder in the distance. We were not prepared for rain and hurried down the hill towards a small hut at the edge of the park. A man there welcomed us and put two chairs near his door for Ada and me.

'Isn't it better inside the hut?'

'Oh no, Esther dear!' said Ada quietly. 'We are fine here.'

Ada replied to me, but I had not spoken. My heart began to race again. I had never heard the voice, as I had never seen the face until that day in church, but it affected me in the same strange way. Again, pictures of my sad past came into my mind.

'I have frightened you?' Lady Dedlock asked. She had also escaped from the storm by coming to this small building and now stood behind my chair. 'I believe,' she continued, 'that I have the pleasure of speaking to Mr John Jarndyce. I saw you in church, but because of Sir Leicester's disagreement with

your friend, Mr Boythorn, I was not able to speak to you.'

My guardian took Lady Dedlock's hand and greeted her warmly. Then he introduced Ada and me to his old friend.

'These young ladies are very fortunate to have you as their guardian. A long time has passed since we were in the habit of meeting, Mr Jarndyce, but I think you knew my sister better than you knew me?' said Lady Dedlock.

'Yes, we often met many years ago.'

After the storm passed, a carriage arrived at the hut with Lady Dedlock's two maids: Rosa and Hortense.

'Why are there two of you?' asked Lady Dedlock. 'I only asked for Rosa.'

'*I* am your maid, madam,' explained Hortense proudly. 'Rosa is only my assistant.'

'Rosa,' replied Lady Dedlock calmly, 'give me my coat and get in the carriage with me. Mr Jarndyce, it has been wonderful to see you, but I am afraid we will not be able to become friends again.'

Hortense silently watched the carriage drive towards Chesney Wold. Then, without a word, she took her shoes off, left them on the ground and walked angrily in the same direction through the wet grass.

'Is that young woman mad?' asked my guardian, watching the maid.

'Oh no, sir,' answered the man in the hut, 'she has a good brain, but she is jealous; she won't be happy to have anyone put above her.'

◆

Back at home in Bleak House, we saw Richard on most Saturdays and Sundays. He was still as kind and loving as ever, but my thoughts about him were not comfortable. His conversations were always about Jarndyce and Jarndyce. He saw Miss Flite at the Court of Chancery daily, and I worried that he was becoming more like her, with nothing on his mind except the destructive case. I looked for an opportunity to talk to him alone.

'Well, Richard,' I began, 'are you working hard and with a clear purpose?'

'No, I can't really say that. Not while we are waiting for a judgement in Jarndyce and Jarndyce.'

'But do you think there will ever be a decision in that case?'

'I have no doubt about it,' answered Richard. 'Esther, I know you are worried about me. I didn't work hard enough with Mr Badger, or at Kenge and Carboy, and I know it was wrong of me to get into **debt**, and ...'

'Richard, *are* you in debt?'

'Yes, I am a little, my dear, and I hope you don't hate me for that. But I know

---

debt /det/ (n) money that you must pay back to someone. A *debtor* is someone who has borrowed money and has not paid it back.

our case will be decided soon, and then everything will be all right. I will marry Ada, and we will have a happy life together.'

I watched as the tears fell from Richard's eyes. He was tired and worried.

'Richard, have you finished at Kenge and Carboy?' I asked. 'You said you *didn't* work hard there.'

'I think I have had enough of the law, but I know what profession I want to go into. I am certain about this one: the army – and it won't be for life. When the suit is decided, I won't need a job, but the army will suit me for now.'

In the next weeks, my guardian had many long conversations with Richard about his future, and finally agreed to help him enter the army as an officer. Soon Richard received his orders, but before he left us again, Mr Jarndyce had a very serious meeting with him.

After the two cousins had finished talking, our guardian asked Ada and me to join them.

'We have had a friendly difference of opinion, and I must explain it to you because you are the subject, Ada. My dear, Rick has no money, and he must prove that he can make a success of himself in the army. He must stop thinking that he will be rich one day because of Jarndyce and Jarndyce. That suit has brought only disaster to everyone who has placed their hopes in it.'

Richard bit his lip and held his breath.

'Ada, my dear,' said Mr Jarndyce after he had calmed down, 'my advice to you and Rick is to be cousins again and nothing more. Give yourselves time, and everything may work out as you hope.'

'Cousin Richard,' said Ada sadly, 'we should listen to our guardian. My love for you will never die, but for now, you are my cousin and nothing more. I hope with all my heart that you find success in the army.'

From that day, Richard's feelings towards Mr Jarndyce changed. He was never able to forgive him. I was sad that he left London without returning to the old relationship he had had with his cousin and guardian.

3.1 Were you right?

Look at your answers to Activity 2.4. Find examples of the eight points of style from either Chapter 3 or 4 and write them in your notebook.

1 *Verbs in present time, Chapter 3*
   When she *hears* the name of Sir Leicester's lawyer, Mrs Rouncewell *agrees* that Rosa *can* show the house to the men, and Watt happily *follows*.

3.2 What more did you learn?

1 Draw lines between the two characters in the centre and five people that they are each connected to in Chapters 3 and 4.

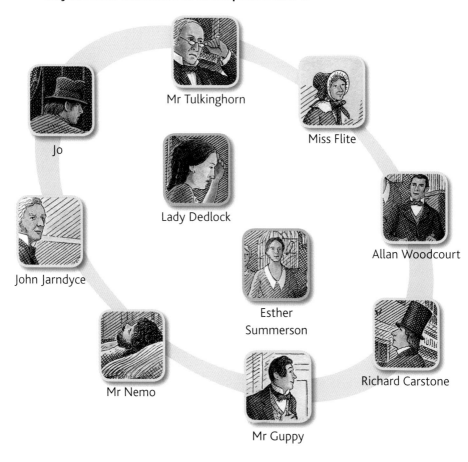

Mr Tulkinghorn

Miss Flite

Jo

Lady Dedlock

Allan Woodcourt

John Jarndyce

Esther Summerson

Mr Nemo

Richard Carstone

Mr Guppy

2 Discuss with other students what you know about these connections. Is there any connection between the two women in the centre?

3.3 Language in use

Look at the sentences in the box. Then circle the best words in *italics* to make the page from Richard's diary more interesting.

> Hortense is **horribly** jealous.
>
> I became **quite** angry with myself.

When I was growing up I always felt ¹*brightly / awfully* lonely because I didn't have any brothers or sisters. Then, when I was nineteen, my life became ²*a little / very much* better because I met my ³*unbelievably / stupidly* generous cousin, Mr John Jarndyce, and my ⁴*strangely / wonderfully* beautiful cousin, Miss Ada Clare. In addition I met Esther Summerson, an ⁵*equally / annoyingly* beautiful and generous friend.

I was ⁶*perfectly / anxiously* happy in my new home, Bleak House, but soon I had to think about a profession and begin to work hard ⁷*freely / enough* at my studies to get a good job. I became ⁸*horribly / handsomely* bored with my studies because I was always ⁹*badly / deeply* interested in the case of Jarndyce and Jarndyce in the Court of Chancery. Mr Jarndyce was ¹⁰*clearly / blindly* upset with me but always ¹¹*surprisingly / bleakly* patient and ¹²*boringly / cheerfully* good to me.

3.4 What happens next?

Write the name of the character from Activity 3.2 who you think is most likely to:

1 be controlled by people with power. ....

2 search for facts about the life and death of Mr Nemo. ....

3 have a real name that is different from the one he is known by. ....

4 look for ways to win Esther Summerson's heart. ....

5 feel upset by information from the past. ....

6 realise she has romantic feelings for Mr Woodcourt. ....

CHAPTER 5

Dead or Alive?

'There she is!' cries Jo. 'The fine lady that gave me the money.
I know that veil and coat, and she's the right size.'

During the four summer months, the Court of Chancery is open for only a few hours every day, and the important people – judges, lawyers, even suitors – have gone to more interesting places across the face of the earth, from the south coast of England to the mountains of Nepal.

Because the city is so empty, Mr Snagsby is surprised when his dinner is interrupted by a loud knock on the door. He hurries down to the shop and finds a policeman, Mr Guppy and young Jo at his door.

'This boy,' the policeman begins, 'says you know him. He refuses to move away from the street, although I have told him to go many times.'

'I've been moving away ever since I was born,' cries the boy, drying his dirty tears on his arm. 'I don't have no place to move away *to*.'

'I know the boy, and he is no trouble to anyone,' says Mr Snagsby kindly.

'Good evening, Mr Snagsby.' Mr Guppy finally speaks. 'I heard Jo say your name when I was passing, so I thought I would lead the policeman here.'

'But he must move five kilometres away from here,' says the policeman. 'And he has too much money in his pockets for a boy in rags. He says he was given it by a lady, but he can't expect me to believe that story.'

'I don't expect nothing, sir, and I don't know nothing,' cries Jo.

'Officer,' begins Mr Snagsby, 'Jo will move away. He is a good boy.'

After the policeman has left, Mr Snagsby and Mr Guppy question Jo about the fine lady and his gold coin. Mr Guppy is becoming a little like the great Mr Tulkinghorn and keeps the details of Jo's story safely in his head, ready for future use.

◆

Mr Guppy and the new law student, Mr Richard Carstone, are the only workers in the offices of Kenge and Carboy during this hot, lazy summer. Richard, who has not yet left the law to join the army, spends his days studying the Jarndyce and Jarndyce papers.

Guppy is bored, so he is very pleased when his old friend Tony Jobling appears at the office. Jobling used to work in another legal office in London, but had to leave for rather mysterious reasons. He wants to be in the city again, and has come to ask for help from his good friend.

'Jobling! Wonderful to see you, old man! Let's go to lunch. I shall pay!'

After a good meal and several glasses of beer, Jobling says, 'I can't believe how poor I find myself today.'

'Well, Tony, you were taking chances with other people's money.'

'Guppy, I will not deny it, but I got caught, and now I have no job and not a penny to my name.'

'You could copy legal documents for Snagsby until you find a better job. Wait! There is more to my plan. Krook, at the Rag and Bottle Market, has a room for rent at an affordable price. You could get friendly with him.'

'Why would I want to do that?' asks Jobling.

'He is old and usually drunk and almost always alone, so we might discover his secrets one day. Some people say he is enormously rich. Who knows what you might find out?'

After the two friends drink to the plan, Guppy quietly adds, 'Krook's last tenant died there. You don't mind that, do you?'

'Well, I think that wasn't very polite, but let's go and talk to old Krook and see the room,' suggests Jobling.

The two young men find Krook still sleeping at one o'clock in the afternoon, and have a hard time waking him up.

'How do you do, Mr Krook,' shouts Guppy. 'I hope you are well!'

'Hi! Guppy!' Krook finally answers. Then he looks at his empty alcohol bottle and says, 'Has somebody finished my drink?'

'Not us,' says Guppy. 'But I shall get you another bottle from next door.'

Guppy returns almost immediately with a full bottle of alcohol which Krook accepts very happily. 'You are a true gentleman, Guppy.'

Guppy takes advantage of this friendly mood and soon Jobling has rented Mr Nemo's old room. The young men hurry to Mr Snagsby's house and are successful there, too.

◆

Not long after poor Jo's visit to Mr Snagsby's shop, Mr Tulkinghorn invites Snagsby to dinner. The lawyer wants to discover more details about the boy's meeting with the lady who was asking about Nemo. Tulkinghorn's second guest is Mr Bucket, a private detective.

'Mr Bucket has heard about this business and has some questions for the boy,' explains Mr Tulkinghorn. 'Help him find Jo and bring him here.'

Snagsby seems upset at this suggestion, but Mr Bucket understands what he is thinking. 'The boy will be paid for his trouble, and I promise he will be all right. We have a few questions about Mr Nemo. Perhaps he owned a little property or had some money hidden away. We want to find out if this female is looking for something that does not belong to her.'

'Oh, I see,' says Snagsby although he is not sure that he does.

Mr Bucket and Snagsby finally find Jo delivering some medicine to a poor woman. He has moved away from his usual places and found a place to sleep near the brick-makers. Of course he does not understand what is happening, but follows Mr Snagsby, who has always been kind to him.

In Tulkinghorn's office the lights have been turned down and there is a woman in a long dark coat with a veil over her face standing in the centre of the room when Jo and the two men enter.

'There she is!' cries Jo. 'The fine lady that gave me the money. I know that veil and coat, and she's the right size.'

'Jo,' says Bucket, 'are you certain that she is the lady? Look at her hands.'

'Oh. Those aren't her hands – they were whiter and smaller, and her rings were very beautiful.'

'Listen to her voice, Jo,' says Bucket. And then the lady speaks.

'No, it can't be her. That's not her voice and those aren't her hands, but the veil and the coat are hers. I'm sure about that.'

When Jo has gone, the woman lifts her veil.

'Thank you, Miss Hortense,' says Mr Tulkinghorn.

'Sir, kindly remember that I am now not employed by Lady Dedlock,' the Frenchwoman begins. 'I hope you may be able to help me.'

'I will do whatever I can. I wish you good night,' says Mr Tulkinghorn very formally. 'And to you, Snagsby.'

'Without doubt,' says Bucket, 'the other woman was dressed in the Frenchwoman's clothes on the night she asked Jo to be her guide.'

◆

Mr Tulkinghorn continues his own detective work. Before talking to Jo, he knew that Lady Dedlock wanted to discover more about Mr Nemo. His search has uncovered the possibility that Nemo's real name was Captain Hawdon.

Tulkinghorn has Nemo's signature from Snagsby, but he needs to match it with an example of Captain Hawdon's writing.

Mr Bucket has learned that Hawdon was in the army with Mr George Rouncewell, the owner of a London training school for men who want to learn the skills of real soldiers. He has also discovered that Mr Rouncewell has borrowed money from Mr Smallweed, a clever and terribly greedy old money-lender who sometimes does little jobs for Tulkinghorn. Bucket tells Smallweed to bring Mr Rouncewell to Tulkinghorn's office for an interview.

'Mr Rouncewell,' says Tulkinghorn, not pausing to greet the old soldier politely, 'I understand that you served in the army with Captain Hawdon, and that you were good friends. Perhaps you have a note or a letter in Captain Hawdon's handwriting. I wish to compare his writing with an example of writing that I have. Perhaps this is something you could lend me?'

'I have no experience of business, and when I hear you talk, I feel that I can't breathe. I am not the equal of you gentlemen, but if you will allow me to ask, why do you need to see something in the captain's handwriting?'

'I cannot tell you. But I will say that this bit of business will not harm Captain Hawdon,' says Tulkinghorn.

'Of course not. He is dead,' says George Rouncewell.

'*Is* he?' asks the lawyer as he returns to his desk.

'Yes, he went over the side of a ship, and may he rest in peace,' says George. 'You won't explain yourself, so I will not be part of this business.'

'Good day, Mr Rouncewell. Don't forget to make your payments to Mr Smallweed on time. You don't want to have any trouble with the police.'

On hearing these rude words, George Rouncewell hurries out of Tulkinghorn's office. 'What an awful man! A murderous, dangerous, nasty sort of man!' he says to himself as he rushes angrily out of the building.

Unfortunately, Tulkinghorn's servant hears these words as he passes Rouncewell on the stairs.

◆

It is autumn and Sir Leicester and his wife are at their house in town. One evening, Lady Dedlock's quiet reading is interrupted by a servant: 'The young man, My Lady, of the name of Guppy,' he says.

'Mr Guppy, you are, of course, the person who has written me so many letters?' asks Lady Dedlock without greeting Guppy.

'Yes, madam, several, but today my business is too important, and too private, to put in writing. Have you, madam, ever heard of or seen a young lady of the name Miss Esther Summerson?'

'I saw a young lady of that name not long ago,' answers Lady Dedlock.

'I have visited Chesney Wold, and when I saw your picture above the fireplace, I noticed that you and Miss Summerson are very similar.'

Lady Dedlock gives Guppy one of her coldest looks and says, 'Why do you think your opinion of my picture is of any interest to me?'

'Madam, if I could solve the mystery of Miss Summerson's birth, she might begin to admire me and might then agree to marry me. From papers at Kenge and Carboy,' continues Guppy politely, 'I learned that Miss Barbary, Miss Summerson's aunt, looked after her when she was a child. Does Miss Barbary have a connection to your family?'

Lady Dedlock's face has gone very pale. 'I know the name.'

'Miss Barbary told Mr Kenge that the girl's last name was really Hawdon.'

Lady Dedlock is shocked and has to force herself to stay calm.

'Madam, there is one final point. Some time ago, a law-writer was found dead at the house of a person named Krook, near Chancery Lane. I have discovered recently that the dead man's real name was Hawdon.'

'And is *that* my business?'

'Later, a lady hired a poor sweeping boy to show her the final resting place of Hawdon, or Nemo, as he was known. The boy knows the lady's voice and can describe her hands and her rings. The police believe that Nemo left nothing behind in his room when he died. But he did. He left a packet of old letters, and tomorrow night I will have those letters in my hand. I have explained my purpose, and if you agree, I will bring these letters here tomorrow night and look at them for the first time with you.'

Lady Dedlock is not certain that she can believe this young man, but she answers, again calmly, 'You may bring the letters if you choose.'

When My Lady is alone, she falls to her knees and a horrible cry shakes her whole body. 'Oh, my child, my child! Not dead in the first hours of her life! My cruel sister lied to me and stole my child from me!'

◆

Tony Jobling has become friends with Krook, often bringing him a bottle of his favourite alcohol. Krook has agreed to show Tony the packet of letters that he took from Mr Nemo's suitcase on the night the law-writer died. Guppy hopes that the information in these letters will help him to win Esther Summerson's love. He arrives at Jobling's room just after ten o'clock.

'There is something strange in the air tonight,' says Tony Jobling.

'You are right. Is there a chimney on fire? Something smells horrible. There are little pieces of black stuff on your table and on our clothes. I can't brush them off. It seems like some kind of fat,' complains Guppy.

'Let's open the window and breathe some air,' suggests Jobling.

Finally, at midnight, Jobling goes downstairs, but he returns in seconds.

'Have you got the letters?' shouts Guppy.

'No,' says Jobling. 'Krook's not there. I opened his door and there was a terrible burning smell, and I could see the same black stuff and yellow oil that we saw up here on the walls and table, but no old man.'

The two young men hurry down the stairs to find Krook.

'Look!' says Jobling. 'There is his hat on the back of his chair. And there on the floor is the red string that was around the letters.'

The only other thing they find is a small, burnt, oily mark on the floor with something that looks like pieces of white bones resting on it. Suddenly they realise that this is what is left of Krook – and they run into the street, more frightened than they have ever been in their lives.

Mr Krook has been burned to death by a fire that started inside his own body. It is a very rare way to die, but scientifically, it is not impossible.

CHAPTER 6

Esther's Story: A Mother's Love

Her tears were falling as she fell to her knees and cried, 'My child, my child,
I am your terrible and unhappy mother! Can you forgive me?'

My guardian continued to be a model of kindness and generosity. He regularly – and secretly – sent a small amount of money to Miss Flite after he had met her. And I was surprised when a thirteen-year-old orphan knocked at my door one day and introduced herself by saying, 'I am Charley, miss – your maid. I'm a gift to you, with Mr Jarndyce's love.'

We had met Charley and her younger brother and sister in London after their father had died, making them orphans. Charley went out to work every day and locked six-year-old Tom and baby Emma in their room. After a long day washing clothes for other people, she hurried home to take care of her little family. When Mr Jarndyce made Charley my maid, he sent Tom to school and put the baby in the care of a good family.

One afternoon Charley came to me and asked, 'Miss, do you know a poor person named Jenny?'

'I know a brick-maker's wife by that name,' I answered.

'She came and spoke to me when I was near the doctor's practice.'

'Is she ill?' I asked.

'No, miss, she's looking after a poor boy from London. He helped her once when she needed some medicine, and now he's very ill and she wants to help him. He doesn't have a home and there's no mother or father.'

I could read Charley's thoughts and we were quickly out of the door. At Jenny's house we found the poor boy sitting in a corner, shaking and unable to get warm; a strange, unhealthy smell came from him.

I had not yet lifted my veil, and the boy looked up, clearly frightened. 'I won't take you to that place again. Let Mr Nemo rest in peace.'

'Jo, Jo, what's the matter?' asked Jenny. 'These are friends. They've come to help you. I'm sorry, miss, he's crazy sometimes.'

'She looks like the other one,' Jo said when I lifted my veil. 'She has the face, but a different coat and hat.'

Charley talked to the boy and he calmed down. He was very, very ill, but Jenny could not keep him in her house. She knew that her husband would hit her and throw the boy out if he found him there.

'We will take him with us and try to get some help for him,' I told Jenny.

'Leave me here,' said Jo. 'I can get warm beside the bricks.'

'But people die here,' explained Charley. 'You come with us.'

'They die everywhere. I showed her where Mr Nemo died, and where they put him. If she isn't that lady, who is she?' asked Jo. He was confused, but he followed Charley, and soon we gave him some soup and medicine and put him to bed in a warm room in one of Mr Jarndyce's farm buildings. I was happy to think that the poor boy was safe and comfortable.

But next morning there was bad news. Jo had disappeared in the night. We worried that his illness, probably a very strong fever, had got worse and that he was not in his right mind. We searched everywhere for five days, but we found no sign of him.

The search ended because another worry upset us. Charley was sitting at her worktable in the evening, and I saw that she was shaking from head to foot.

'Charley, are you so cold?' I asked.

'I don't know what it is,' she replied. 'But I think I'm ill, miss.'

I knew that I had to act quickly. I locked the door to my rooms and kept everyone out, but I stayed with Charley and nursed her. Sometimes she knew me, and other times she was not herself and her words made very little sense. She was in danger of death for many days, but not one word of complaint came from her lips and she never lost her gentle, loving nature.

And Charley did not die. She began to grow strong again. It was a great morning when I could tell Ada all this as she stood in the garden under my window; and it was a great evening when Charley and I at last took tea together in my little sitting-room.

But on that same evening I knew that I had caught the fever, and Charley became my nurse. The fever affected me badly, and I was unable to leave my bed. After many days I called Charley to me and said, 'Please come and sit beside me. Hold my hand. Charley, I cannot see you; I am blind.'

I lay ill for several weeks, and the usual habits of my life became like an old memory. I seemed to be on the other side of a dark lake, with all my experiences at a great distance on the healthy shore.

Then, one day, something different happened when I woke up; I could see a small flame from a lamp on the table. I closed my eyes and looked again and it was still there. I had no words for the happiness I felt – I would see again! I did not let my dear Ada enter my room, but now I could read the letters that she wrote to me every morning and evening.

Soon I was sitting at my table and enjoying my first cup of tea with Charley for a long time. 'You are the best nurse I could ever wish for. You have been wonderful to me. But, Charley,' I said, looking round, 'where is my mirror? Surely it should be on that little table in the corner.'

Charley did not answer, but then I knew what had happened. The disease had left its cruel marks on my face. I took her hand and said, 'Charley, you mustn't worry. I am sure that I can do very well without my old face.'

'Dear Esther,' Mr Jarndyce said when he visited me the next morning, 'what a sad time this has been.' I could see that he loved me even without my old face. 'Ada and I have been so worried about you, and poor Rick has written to get news about you. I am afraid he was cold and distant to me in his letters; he believes that I want to steal his rights in Jarndyce and Jarndyce. The case has poisoned his whole life. But, little woman, when can Ada come in?'

I decided that I needed more time before I could see Ada, and asked Mr Jarndyce if Charley and I could go to Mr Boythorn's house for a visit. The fresh air and quiet life would make us both stronger. But before leaving for the countryside, I had one more visitor who I welcomed into my room. Miss Flite had travelled from London to see me when she heard about my illness. As usual, she was full of news. 'My dear, do you know that my carriage to Bleak House was followed by a poor woman in an old hat?'

'It was Jenny, miss,' added Charley. 'She told me that there's been a lady with a veil at her little house asking about your health and taking away your handkerchief – the one you kindly left there when her baby died. Jenny doesn't know the woman and didn't want her to take the handkerchief, but it seemed so important to her.'

'Who can she be?' I said.

But Miss Flite had other news. 'My dear, I don't think you know about Mr Woodcourt, who was my special doctor.'

'But I thought Mr Woodcourt was very far away,' I said.

'Yes, he is, but he has become a great hero. There was a terrible storm at sea, an awful scene. Hundreds of people were dead or dying on the ship. Fire, storm and darkness. Mr Woodcourt stayed calm and brave and saved many lives. The whole country has thanked him. I have the newspaper report here in my bag. I have brought it to show you – he is admired everywhere.'

When I was alone again, I read the newspaper report about Mr Woodcourt. And now I must tell you the little secret that I have kept to myself. Sometimes I imagined that Mr Woodcourt was a rich man and did not have to go away to earn his fortune. In my dreams, he stayed in England and told me that he loved me and I was very happy. But now I was glad that he had gone away. It was better that he was not tied to someone like me, with a ruined face. I could continue along the path of duty, and he could follow his road without me.

◆

During our time at Mr Boythorn's house, everything was done to help Charley and me grow stronger. We stayed in the fresh air all day, climbing every hill and travelling over every road and field in the area, playing with the village children, talking to friends. In the house, I taught Charley about grammar and wrote long letters to Ada. If I did catch sight of my face in a mirror sometimes, I got busy again and tried to forget about it. No one had turned away from me or refused my friendship. I had too much to be thankful for to worry about what I had lost.

Charley and I had a favourite spot where there was a pretty seat under a tree and a lovely view. I was resting on this seat after a long walk, and Charley was picking wild flowers at a little distance from me when I noticed a woman coming towards us through the trees. Little by little, I saw that it was Lady Dedlock, hurrying to where I sat. There was something in her face that I had dreamed of seeing when I was a child – something that I had never seen in any face. But when Charley came to sit beside me, Lady Dedlock was again the proud, fashionable lady of Chesney Wold.

'Miss Summerson, I was upset to hear about your fever. I hope that I haven't frightened you. Are you getting stronger?' she asked kindly.

'I am quite well, Lady Dedlock, thank you,' I replied. I stared at her pale, beautiful face.

'Will you please send your maid home?'

When Charley had left, Lady Dedlock sat down on the seat beside me. I saw in her hand the handkerchief with which I had covered the dead baby.

I looked at her but I could not breathe. My heart was beating so violently and wildly that I believed my life would end at that moment. But then Lady Dedlock put her arms around me and kissed me! Her tears were falling as she fell to her knees and cried, 'My child, my child, I am your terrible and unhappy mother! Can you forgive me?'

I tried to tell her that I had nothing to forgive. I told her that my heart was full of natural love for her, and that nothing could change that. I only asked her for permission to love her as a child loves its mother. We sat with our arms

around each other, but our two troubled minds were not at peace.

'My dear daughter, it is much too late for us to be together. I must travel my dark road alone; I will always be punished for my past and I must always keep this secret and protect my husband, if that is possible.'

My unhappy mother told me that she had not imagined that I was her child until recently. She had come here to have one, and only one, meeting with me.

After that, we would not communicate with each other again on earth, but she had a letter for me, which she asked me to read and then destroy.

'After today, you must think that I am dead, but remember that I love you with a mother's love. I must keep our secret from my husband and from society. I cannot destroy him and his life.'

'But has the secret been kept safe, dearest Mother?' I asked.

'It was almost discovered recently, but it was saved by an accident. Our lawyer, Mr Tulkinghorn, has been trying to discover things about me. He loves to have power over people. He doesn't pity me, and if he gets this information he will use it against me.'

'But, dear Mother, do you have to travel this road alone? Can I not help you?' I didn't want to lose her after finally finding her. I had missed a mother's love all my life.

'My child, my child!' she said. 'For the last time! These kisses and this touch for the last time! We shall meet no more. I will return to my old life and play my part as Lady Dedlock, but I will suffer because I have murdered the only love I have ever felt. Please remember this and forgive me if you can, and ask heaven to forgive me, which it never can!'

She gave me one last kiss and walked away from me. I returned to Mr Boythorn's house and, alone in my own room, I read the letter from Lady Dedlock, my mother. She had not **abandoned** me. She thought that I had died, but her older sister, the godmother of my childhood, had discovered signs of life in my small body. With her strict sense of duty, she had taken me away from my mother and looked after me secretly in her house. Neither of my parents – who were never married to each other – had known that I was still alive.

I burned the letter, worried that I was the cause of the possible disgrace of my mother, and of a proud family name. I fell asleep thinking that my birth was an unwelcome mistake that had caused terrible problems for many people.

But when I woke up, I began to realise how wrong these thoughts were. I had a letter from Ada telling me how happy she was that she would see me soon. And there was another letter from my guardian saying that nobody else could manage the keys, and that everybody said the house was not the same without me. And there were so many other friends and so many happy duties, that soon I understood that I was meant to live. I was not guilty of a crime; I accepted my life and decided to be happy in it.

abandon /əˈbændən/ (v) to leave someone or something for a long time or forever, without intending to go back to them

4.1 Were you right?

Look back at your answers to Activity 3.4. Then correct mistakes in these sentences according to the events in Chapters 5 and 6. Cross out the words that are wrong and write the correct ones.

1   Mr Snagsby orders Jo to move five kilometres away from his usual streets.   ....

2   Mr Bucket is looking for an example of Captain Hawdon's writing.   ....

3   Mr Nemo's surname at birth was Rouncewell.   ....

4   Tony Jobling thinks he might be able to marry Esther Summerson one day if he can help her to discover more about her background.   ....

5   Miss Barbary suffers when she learns that Esther Summerson is really her daughter.   ....

6   Miss Flite has secretly hoped that Allan Woodcourt will fall in love with her.   ....

4.2 What more did you learn?

1   Who do (or did) these belong to? Write the name under each picture.

2   Discuss with other students how each of these things is important to the story.

4.3 **Language in use**

Look at the sentence in the box
and change it to good English. Then
complete these sentences. Write one
word in each space.

> 'I don't expect **nothing**, sir, and I don't
> know **nothing**,' cried Jo.

1 Jo had .... to live.

2 Mr Guppy's friend rented the room .... Mr Nemo died in.

3 Jo helped a woman .... hands were whiter and smaller than
Miss Hortense's.

4 Tulkinghorn wanted .... in Captain Hawdon's handwriting to
compare with Nemo's signature.

5 Tulkinghorn's servant heard George criticising the lawyer to ....
.as he left the building.

6 Lady Dedlock had to control .... when Mr Guppy told her
that Esther's real last name was Hawdon.

7 Mr Guppy and Mr Jobling smelt ...., but they did not know
it was Krook's body burning.

8 Esther and Charley visited Jo, ... was very ill.

9 .... turned away from Esther when they saw her face after
her illness.

10 When Lady Dedlock and Esther met, they sat with their arms around each
....

4.4 **What happens next?**

First look at the titles of Chapters 7 and 8. Then look at the pictures in those
chapters. Discuss how the titles and pictures may be connected.

1 In Chapter 7, who do you think is going to be dishonest: Mr Tulkinghorn or Miss
Hortense?

2 Who has been dishonest with Jo?

3 In Chapter 8, what changes do you think might be coming for Richard, Mr Guppy
and Esther Summerson?

Dishonest Business

*'Sir Leicester, his family history, his position in society and his good name
cannot be separated. We must find a way to protect your husband.'*

After Krook's mysterious death, the neighbours are surprised to see two very
old people move into the Rag and Bottle Market. They are Mr Smallweed,
the money-lender, and his wife, Mr Krook's sister.

After Krook's death and the disappearance of the packet of letters, Mr Guppy
has lost hope of discovering more about Miss Esther Summerson's background.
With a sad heart, he returns to Lady Dedlock's London house.

'Lady Dedlock,' begins Guppy politely, 'I have come to report that I have not
been able to get the letters which we spoke about. I believe they were destroyed
in a strange fire when a man named Krook died.'

Tulkinghorn is at the door of the library as Guppy departs. What does he
know about the business between My Lady and this young man?

◆

Soon after the death of Mr Krook, old Mr Smallweed orders Mr George
Rouncewell to pay the total amount of his debt immediately. George's oldest and
best friend, Mr Matthew Bagnet, signed the papers for the **loan** and will have to
pay the debt if George cannot. The two men hurry to Smallweed's home to find
out what is happening, but Smallweed refuses to discuss the matter with them
and sends them to his lawyer.

After making many excuses, Mr Tulkinghorn's servant finally lets George
into the lawyer's office. Mr Bagnet waits anxiously outside.

'Mr Rouncewell, you must pay your debts or accept your punishment. If
you can't pay, then your friend must pay. His signature is on the loan,' says
Tulkinghorn coldly.

'Mr Tulkinghorn, neither of us has this sum of money. Smallweed has
changed the conditions of the loan,' says George angrily. 'I will not ruin my
friend and his family. You wanted a piece of paper from me the other day. I will
give it to you to solve this problem.'

'Mr Rouncewell,' the lawyer begins coolly, 'if you choose to leave your letter
from Captain Hawdon with me, I can return the conditions of your loan to what
they were, and I can free Mr Bagnet from any responsibility towards the loan in
the future. Do you agree?'

The old soldier puts his hand in his pocket and produces a letter from
Hawdon. 'I must,' he says angrily.

loan /ləʊn/ (n) an amount of money that you borrow

◆

Mr Tulkinghorn shares with no one the information that he has about Captain Hawdon until one destructive evening at Chesney Wold.

The gentlemen discuss business and politics after dinner. Sir Leicester is worried that men from a lower social class are entering parliament.

'But, Sir Leicester,' Tulkinghorn informs him, 'a number of these people send their children to good schools now. Many of them own factories or other sorts of businesses. These people are, in their way, very proud.'

'Proud?' Sir Leicester doubts that he has heard correctly.

'Really, Sir Leicester. I am stating facts. I could tell you a true story that I heard recently, with Lady Dedlock's permission,' says Tulkinghorn.

'Of course,' Lady Dedlock replies politely.

'The rich, beautiful wife of a man in a position similar to yours hired a young girl to be her maid. The lady was fond of the girl and acted with great kindness towards her. But the lady had a secret that she had kept to herself for many years. In fact, she had in early life planned to marry a young army captain. Unfortunately, he failed to make a success of his life. The lady never married him, but she gave birth to a child; the army captain was the father.'

Lady Dedlock sits near the window, staring at the stars and not moving.

'The captain was dead, so the lady believed that her secret was safe, but after many years facts about her past began to come out. Her husband's heart was broken, and his life was in pieces. But that is not the point I want to make. When the young girl's father – the *maid's* father – heard about the lady's disgrace, he took his daughter out of the gentleman's house. He didn't want her to have any connection with a woman with that sort of history.'

Sir Leicester is tired and has not followed the story closely; soon he wishes his guest good night.

Mr Tulkinghorn goes to his usual bedroom with a slight smile on his face. He walks up and down his room, satisfied with the evening and with his plans, until he hears a quiet knock at his door.

Lady Dedlock looks very pale. Is it fear or anger? She does not speak at first, but finally says, 'Why have you told my story?'

'It was necessary to inform you that I knew it. I have known all the details for only a few days.'

'Is it true that Rosa's father knows my history? Is *that* true?'

'No, it was a way to interest Sir Leicester in the facts,' Tulkinghorn says.

'I will leave Chesney Wold,' Lady Dedlock begins. 'I have expected this for a long time. I will take nothing from here – no money, no jewels, no clothes – and will put an end to my lies and my secrets.'

'Lady Dedlock, you cannot leave Chesney Wold. You must not. My only thought in this unhappy situation is Sir Leicester. He is a very proud man. He would be more surprised by your fall from your high position as his wife than by the moon falling from the sky.'

'Then isn't it better for me to leave immediately,' asks Lady Dedlock, 'and to protect him from this disgrace?'

'Your flight would advertise your history to the world. It would be impossible to save the family's good name. Sir Leicester, his family history, his position in society and his good name cannot be separated. We must find a way to protect your husband,' advises Tulkinghorn. 'You must continue to live with your guilty secrets until I tell you differently.'

◆

Mr Tulkinghorn does not stay long at Chesney Wold and is soon in his London rooms again. He is looking forward to a fine bottle of wine with his supper the next evening when there is a knock at his door.

'Who's this?' he asks himself, and then finds Miss Hortense, the Frenchwoman, outside. 'What do you want?'

'I have been here very often and have not been allowed to come in,' she complains. 'Sir, you lied to me and used me for your purposes.'

'Miss, you forget that I paid you for what I asked you to do.'

'I do not want your money!' Miss Hortense shouts, and violently throws two coins on the floor. 'Keep your money! You knew that I hated My Lady and you used me to get information about her. Find me a good position! If you refuse to help me, I will come here again and again until you do.'

'Miss Hortense, I advise you to pick up your money and leave. We have laws in this country which protect its citizens. If you continue to come here and annoy me, I will send for the police and they will put you in prison.'

'I do not believe you!' cries Miss Hortense.

'Believe me, miss – it is what I will do. Think twice before you come here again. You lost your place with Lady Dedlock because you were difficult and jealous. Change your ways and stay away from me.'

Miss Hortense leaves Tulkinghorn's house without answering or looking behind her.

The dark night rests heavily on one of the poorest and ugliest parts of London. Some of the houses are falling into the street, which is nothing more than a muddy path. Even the air, like the people here, seems unhealthy and sad.

Allan Woodcourt, sunburned from his recent trip, is walking through this unfortunate area of the city when someone shouts, 'Stop him, stop him!' Then he sees a woman chasing after a dirty boy in rags. The young doctor runs after the boy, thinking that he has robbed the woman, and finally catches him in a narrow road with no exit.

'Jo, it is you,' says Mr Woodcourt. 'Do you remember me? I saw you after Mr Nemo's death. What is happening? What is the problem?'

'Why can't everyone leave me alone?' says Jo, brushing the tears from his face with a dirty hand. 'I didn't do nothing, but everyone moves me away time after time. I want to be with Mr Nemo. He was very good to me.'

Allan Woodcourt turns to the woman and asks, 'Has he robbed you?'

'No, sir. He was very kind and helpful to me. He came to us at St Albans when he was very ill. Then a young woman – a good friend to Jo and to me – pitied him and took him to her home. But he thanked her by running away in the middle of the night, and no one could find him until tonight when I saw him. And that kind young lady caught his fever and lost her beauty. Her face has changed, but she still has her sweet voice and her pretty shape and her kind temper. She is still good to everyone who meets her. Even to ungrateful boys like Jo!'

The boy is crying now. 'Sir, I didn't run away. Someone came and took me away, but I'm not allowed to say his name.'

'But why did he want to take you away?' asks the doctor.

'I don't know nothing. He put me in a hospital and told me to stay away from London when I came out, but where could I go? He'll find me again – I know he will,' cries Jo softly. 'But I'm sorry about the pretty woman. I didn't mean to hurt her. I hope she's all right again.'

'Now Jo,' says Allan Woodcourt after hearing Jo's story about his illness, about the mysterious woman in the veil and about the visit to Tulkinghorn's office, 'I am going to find you a better place to rest. Can you follow me?'

As the sun comes up, the doctor and the tired boy walk into a part of London where the air is purer and the streets are cleaner. Mr Woodcourt stops for food and medicine for the boy, and then decides to look for Miss Flite, who might know of a place where Jo can rest and hide.

After a friendly welcome, Miss Flite proudly says that she can solve this problem. 'Mr George Rouncewell will help us! I often visit Mr Rouncewell. He knows your friend, Miss Esther Summerson, and takes a great interest in anyone connected to her. And his place is not far from here.'

Mr Rouncewell is kind and generous and very happy to help a friend of Miss Summerson's or Miss Flite's. The old lady hurries off to the Court of Chancery, and Jo is soon washed and put to bed. Then the two men have time for a little conversation.

'Who is the boy afraid of?' asks Mr Rouncewell.

'He wanted to keep the name secret, but he finally told me that it is someone called Bucket,' says Woodcourt.

'I have had some business with Bucket, the detective,' replies Rouncewell. 'You don't want to have him after you. He is a dangerous type. And I know the office near the Court of Chancery where Bucket took Jo earlier. It is Tulkinghorn's place. I am sorry to say that I know both of these men, and have had nothing but trouble from them.'

'What kind of man is this Tulkinghorn?' asks Mr Woodcourt.

'He is a man without any human feeling. He has caused me greater suffering than all other men put together. He enjoys having power over me – and over a lot of other people, I believe. But if we were in a war and I could attack him fairly, he would die, sir!'

Mr Allan Woodcourt reports everything that he has learned from Jo and from Mr George Rouncewell to Mr John Jarndyce, and very soon both Mr Jarndyce and Miss Esther Summerson visit poor Jo. Esther is wonderfully kind and explains to Jo that she understands why he left Bleak House and that she knows her illness was not his fault.

Jo's health continues to grow worse, but in the warm, comfortable bed at the training school he is happier than he has ever been. Mr Rouncewell is cheerful with him every day, and he knows that Miss Summerson has forgiven him for bringing the fever into her house. With George Rouncewell and Mr Woodcourt at his bedside, Jo often talks about Mr Nemo.

'It's time to go to my resting place beside Mr Nemo,' says Jo. He looks at the doctor. 'I want to tell him that I'm as poor as him now and have come to lie beside him. Will you promise to put me there, beside him, sir?'

'I will, Jo. I promise.'

'The dark night is coming fast now, sir,' says Jo. 'Let me catch hold of your hand, please. I can't see you now.'

'Jo, can you say the words that I say? Say "Our Father, in heaven."'

'Our Father, in heaven – is the light coming, sir?' asks Jo.

'It is close now, Jo.'

'Our Father ...'

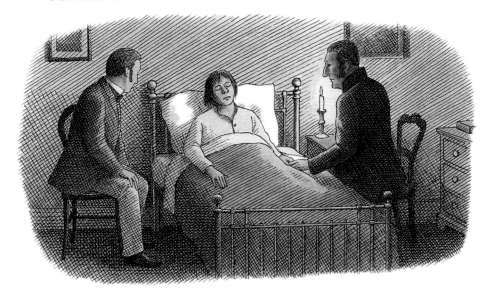

Dead. A poor boy who lived on this earth with no one and nothing. Will he now rest in peace and find the care and kindness that he missed every day of his short life?

CHAPTER 8

Esther's Story: Changes

'Duty, Esther, and if you are not happy to do it cheerfully, through good times and bad, you ought to be. That is all I have to say to you, my dear!'

Ada and Mr Jarndyce joined us at Mr Boythorn's house for a final happy month, and the time passed very quickly. One evening Charley appeared and asked me to step outside with her.

'Excuse me, miss,' she whispered, 'you're wanted at the Dedlock Arms. It's a gentleman, miss. He sends you his good wishes and asks you to come to the pub without saying anything to the others. Mr Grubble came from the pub and gave me the message for you.'

I went to the pub to find out if there was some trouble or if someone needed my help. When I entered the main room, I saw Richard immediately.

'My dear Esther!' he said. 'My dearest, my best friend!'

I lifted my veil and Richard's friendly smile stayed the same. Our friendship was not affected by the changes to my face.

'Dear girl,' Richard said happily. 'My greatest wish is to talk to you because I want you to understand me.'

'And I want you to understand someone else,' I said.

'We must talk about Mr Jarndyce, Esther. I know that you want me to understand *him*. So, let me say first of all that I am twenty-one now, and I do not have to answer to Mr John Jarndyce or to anyone else for my actions.'

His attitude was painful to me and he saw that I looked upset.

'I am sorry – I did not come here to upset you. Let's talk of something else. Am I welcome at Mr Boythorn's house? I would love to see my dear Ada.'

'You are certainly welcome, as always. And how do you like your profession by now?' I asked.

'It is good enough for a time. I don't know that I shall care about it when our suit is decided, but then I can pay to leave the army. I have some free time now, so I have been to the Court of Chancery to look after my interests, but don't worry, I will not talk about our case tonight.'

We hurried back to Mr Boythorn's house and surprised Ada. I could see from her face that she loved him with all her heart. But I have to say that I was less sure about Richard's love for Ada. It seemed that it had to wait until there was a judgement in Jarndyce and Jarndyce.

◆

I met Richard again the next morning and we two walked to my favourite seat. 'One day I would like to rest and relax in a place like this,' Richard said.

'Why don't you rest now?' I asked. 'You are on holiday.'

'There is no rest for suitors in the Court of Chancery.'

'My dear Richard,' I said, 'this is a bad beginning to our conversation. This suit is ruining your life.'

'Those sound like Mr John Jarndyce's words. My dear Esther, how can you be so blind? Don't you see that he wants me to know nothing about Jarndyce and Jarndyce because he doesn't want me to understand it and to have a greater share in the judgement?'

'Richard, Mr Jarndyce has always wanted what is best for you.'

'But Esther, you can see that the case has changed me. Isn't it possible that it has changed Mr Jarndyce, too? The Court of Chancery changes everybody. Why should *he* escape from its power? And now I have reached the age of twenty-one and I can do what pleases me – and it pleases me to look after my own interests. The fact is that my road and Mr Jarndyce's road are not the same. Under one of the wills, I would receive a greater share than he would. I don't think that he would support that will.'

'But is there any justice in this case, Richard?'

'There is justice somewhere in it, Esther. I have studied it for a long time and I am going to do everything possible to get a judgement in our suit. I have made it the purpose of my life. It can't last forever.'

'Richard, I am frightened for you,' I said.

'Don't be. I know what I am doing. But please explain to Ada that although

I cannot see her often at the present time, I am looking after her interests as well as my own. She is still a ward of Court, but when she is older she and I can make our own decisions about our relationship to each other.'

'Richard, I have one question: are you in debt again?'

'Of course I am,' he answered. 'Debts are necessary when you are a suitor in Chancery, but I shall be all right.'

After our meeting, Richard hurried back to London to be in court that afternoon. I returned to Ada and gently tried to explain Richard's situation to her. I think she understood him better than anyone and was willing to do anything to help him. My dear girl told me that night that her unchanging heart would give him as much love as he needed.

◆

When we returned to Bleak House, I felt healthy and strong and received a wonderful welcome from everyone. I found the housekeeping keys waiting for me, gave them a shake and said, 'Duty, Esther, and if you are not happy to do it cheerfully, through good times and bad, you ought to be. That is all I have to say to *you*, my dear!'

After putting the house in order, I arranged to take a short trip to London alone. I had one final piece of business that I wanted to take care of for my mother, and I wanted to finish it as soon as possible. I sent a letter to the offices of Kenge and Carboy and arranged to meet with Mr Guppy privately.

'Miss Summerson, I think of you often and am always very happy to see you,' Mr Guppy greeted me warmly.

'Mr Guppy, you asked me once if you could speak to me and be confident that our conversation would be private. I would like to ask if you would do the same thing for me now.'

'Miss Summerson, it is my pleasure to do anything for you.'

When I lifted the veil from my face, Mr Guppy suddenly could not speak and looked totally confused and embarrassed.

'Miss Summerson,' he said quietly, 'you have just spoken about a meeting when I – when I asked you to ... ' The next words seemed to stick in his throat, and he coughed, made faces and looked around the room.

Finally he began again. 'At that meeting you very politely refused my request. I hope you remember that you said "no" to me.'

'There can be no doubt, Mr Guppy, that I thanked you and told you that I could never marry you. I have not changed my mind about that decision.'

'Yes, that is what happened, and that was an end to the discussion, the final word on the matter, was it not?' asked Mr Guppy anxiously.

'Mr Guppy, I accept your view of that meeting without question.'

'Thank you, miss – thank you for understanding that I could never repeat my request,' said Guppy quickly.

'May I now say what I wished to say to you?' I began. 'I know everything I need to know about my personal history, and I would like you to abandon any searches into it. Would you please do this for me, for my peace of mind?'

'Miss Summerson, I apologise for thinking you were here for any other reason, and I am most happy to follow your wishes.'

I could see that Mr Guppy was ashamed of his earlier thoughts, but now we understood each other and said goodbye in a friendly way.

◆

I took all my troubles to my guardian and told him what I now knew of my background. With a clear understanding of my feelings, he spoke gently and wisely to me and agreed to help me keep my mother's secret from the world. I had never loved him so dearly, never thanked him in my heart so fully. Before I fell asleep that night, I wondered if I could ever be good enough to show him how much his love and care meant to me.

The next morning we talked again about the danger which surrounded my mother and about how we could help protect her from disgrace. Of course, I would stay away from her so no one would recognise a connection between us, but possibly there were already people who had thought of such a relationship. First there was the lawyer, Tulkinghorn, who my mother feared.

'Tulkinghorn is very dangerous,' Mr Jarndyce said. 'But allow me to repeat myself, Esther – you are innocent in all of this, and you cannot affect the actions of people like this lawyer. Remember that from today I will share your secret and do everything I can to help you with your worries.'

What could I ever do but thank him! I was going out of the door when he asked me to stay a moment.

'My dear Esther,' said my guardian, 'I have had something in my thoughts for a long time that I have wished to say to you, but I find it difficult to speak about it. Would you allow me to write to you about it?'

'Guardian, of course. You could never offend me in anything you do.'

'Dear girl, give me your hand,' replied Mr Jarndyce. 'You have changed me and my home from the day you arrived. You have made me happy.'

'Guardian! You have done so much for *me* since that time!' I cried.

'But don't think of that now. You must remember that nothing can change me as you know me. I cannot write my letter unless you promise me that this is true. If you doubt that in any way, I will not write the letter, but if you can understand this point and promise me, you can send Charley to me in one week to collect "the letter".'

◆

One week later, Charley placed Mr Jarndyce's letter on the table in my room and left me alone. Before I opened it, I thought of my lonely childhood and of the happiness that I had found since Mr Jarndyce came into my life.

Then I opened the letter and read about my guardian's love for me and his careful thoughts about my feelings and about my future. It was written as he always spoke to me, and I felt his kind protectiveness in every word, every line. Mr John Jarndyce asked me to be his wife, the lady of Bleak House.

He asked me to think about the difference in our ages, and about the fact that Ada would leave Bleak House one day. He also repeated that nothing would change between us if I refused his offer. But how could I refuse? I wanted to help my guardian in any way I could; I wanted to continue to make Bleak House a happy home for him. I wanted to thank him for everything he had done for me.

I cried very much; not only because my heart was full of love, and not because the idea of becoming Mr Jarndyce's wife was strange to me, but because there was something which I could not describe, which was lost to me. I was very happy, very thankful, very hopeful; but I cried.

Then I looked in my mirror and said, 'You will be the lady of Bleak House and you will be happy with your friends, happy in this home, happy doing good, and happy in the love of the best of men.' I gave my keys a shake and thought that my tears were very silly, but I had one more thing to do.

I still had Mr Woodcourt's flowers. I had dried them and put them in a book, but now they were part of something past and gone. I threw them into the fire, and they turned to dust in a minute.

A few days later, when we were alone together, I said in a shaky voice, 'Guardian, when would you like the answer to your letter?'

'When it is ready, my dear,' he replied.

I put my two arms round his neck and kissed him.

'Is this the lady of Bleak House?' he asked.

'Yes,' I answered. And then our life continued in the most normal way.

◆

Unfortunately we continued to worry about Richard. Richard had hired a lawyer, and this man told us that Richard had serious financial problems and had failed to pay him, among others, a large amount of money.

'You know, Esther, Rick will not accept help from me now,' Mr Jarndyce said. 'Could I ask you to visit him and find out about his situation?'

My guardian, Ada and I discussed my trip, and Ada gave me a long letter for Richard before I left for the south coast.

I arrived at the army station and found Richard's apartment in a great mess. Clothes, books, boots, brushes and suitcases covered the floor. Richard was not wearing his army uniform, and his hair and clothes looked as wild as his room, but he said how happy he was to see me.

'I was writing a letter to you,' he said, 'but I am sure you can look at this room and guess what I was going to say. I am finished here.'

'Richard, surely things aren't so bad.'

'Esther, it is hopeless. The army has followed the same route as the other professions; I am in debt and I am not a good soldier. I cannot give my attention to anything except our case in the Court of Chancery – it is the only important thing in my life. I know I sound mad, but we must have a judgement so I can begin my life.'

I did not know what to say, so I handed him Ada's letter.

He read it and turned his face away from me and cried. Finally he looked at me and said, 'She wants to give me the small amount of money that was left to her by her parents. She will receive it when she becomes twenty-one. Oh, Esther, she is so good, and this is the heart that your John Jarndyce has separated me from! Perhaps he suggested this gift so he can use money to keep me away from Bleak House!'

'Richard! I will not listen to you speak about Mr Jarndyce in this way!'

'Please forgive me,' Richard said. 'I am so tired ... but if I had Ada's money, I could make things right, and then Ada and I could be together.'

We studied Richard's papers and saw that he could leave for London with me and arrange the business of coming out of the army from there.

On my way back to my hotel, I saw a crowd of people at the port and joined them to see what was happening. A large ship had arrived from India and the passengers were coming to shore; suddenly I saw Allan Woodcourt, but I was not brave enough to speak to him with my changed face. I knew that I could not behave this way, and said to myself, 'You are no worse than you ever were, and there is no reason for you to hide from a friend.'

When Mr Woodcourt arrived at the hotel, I spoke to him immediately. 'I am pleased to welcome you home. You are a great hero. I heard about your adventure from Miss Flite when I was getting better after a serious illness.'

'Ah, Miss Flite, is she all right?'

'Yes, just the same, and she always remembers you and the help you gave her. She is proud to know you. She is a very loving person.'

'Yes ... you think so?' he replied. I could see that it was difficult for him to speak because he was so sorry for me. 'I was very sorry to hear that you were ill. Are you feeling strong and healthy again?'

'I am my old self again, and you know how good my guardian is to me, and what a happy life we lead. I have everything to be thankful for.'

Then we talked about his voyage and the great storm. Unfortunately he had not made his fortune in India and had come home as poor as when he left. As we were speaking, Richard came in and the two of them were very pleased to greet each other. But when Mr Woodcourt asked Richard about his profession, it was clear that Richard was troubled.

When I was alone for a few minutes with Mr Woodcourt, he spoke to me again. 'Our friend Richard has changed since I last saw him; he seems very worried and anxious.'

'Mr Woodcourt, he is in trouble, and more than anything he needs a friend. I hope that you will see him when you return to London. You cannot imagine how Ada, Mr Jarndyce and I would thank you for this kindness.'

'I promise that I will see him as soon as I am in London.'

When Richard and I were leaving, I looked back at Mr Woodcourt and could see that he was very sorry for me. I felt that my old self was dead now, but I was glad that the kind doctor had not forgotten me.

5.1 Were you right?

Think back to your answers to Activity 4.4. Then mark each of the sentences below T (true) or F (false).

1 ☐ Mr Tulkinghorn sometimes spies on people.

2 ☐ Mr Smallweed's treatment of debtors is always fair.

3 ☐ Miss Hortense has a friendly relationship with Mr Tulkinghorn.

4 ☐ Jo is often forced to leave places.

5 ☐ Richard's love for both Mr Jarndyce and Ada never changes.

6 ☐ One young man does not want to marry Esther; and one old one does.

7 ☐ Richard prefers to stay in the army for many more years.

8 ☐ Esther believes that Allan Woodcourt pities her.

5.2 What more did you learn?

1 Number these events in Esther's life in the order they really happened.

a ☐ Esther visits Jo at George Rouncewell's training school.

b ☐ Esther has a meeting with Mr Guppy in London.

c ☐ Esther welcomes Allan Woodcourt on his return to England.

d ☐1☐ Esther and Charley go to Mr Boythorn's house after their illness.

e ☐ Esther delivers a letter from Ada to Richard at his army station.

f ☐ Esther meets Richard privately near Mr Boythorn's house.

2 Discuss the order of events with other students. Is it difficult to follow the story when events are not reported in the order they really happened? Why do you think this happens in *Bleak House*?

5.3 Language in use

Look at the sentences in the box.
Then re-write the sentences below
using passive verb forms.

> Our friendship **was not affected** by
> the changes to my face.
>
> I have been here very often and **have
> not been allowed** to come in.

1 A fire at Mr Krook's destroyed Lady Dedlock's letters.
   .... Lady Dedlock's letters were destroyed by a fire at Mr Krook's ....

2 Mr Rouncewell's friend signed the loan from Mr Smallweed.
   The loan from Mr Smallweed ....
   ....

3 Mr Smallweed has changed the conditions of the loan.
   The conditions of the loan ....
   ....

4 Mr Tulkinghorn tells Sir Leicester an imaginary story.
   Sir Leicester ....
   ....

5 Her parents left Ada some money.
   Ada ....
   ....

6 Mr Jarndyce has invited Esther to be the lady of Bleak House.
   Esther ....
   ....

5.4 What happens next?

Draw a line between the characters in the box and the adjectives that describe
the type of behaviour you expect from them.

| cruel and controlling | anxious and ashamed | protective and proud | businesslike and energetic | kind and loyal |

> Sir Leicester   Richard   Mr Jarndyce   Mr Tulkinghorn
> Esther   Allan Woodcourt   Lady Dedlock   Ada   Mr Bucket

| weak and self-destructive | brave and skilful | loving but worried | generous and forgiving |

CHAPTER 9

The End of Lies

'Miss Hortense wanted to blame Lady Dedlock for the murder.'
'Lies!' shouts the Frenchwoman. 'It is all lies!'

My Lady has her dinner alone this evening in the Dedlocks' London house; she has much on her mind. Her thoughts are interrupted by a servant who tells her that Mr Tulkinghorn is in the house and wishes to speak to her.

'Lady Dedlock, have you sent your maid – Rosa, I believe her name is – back to the village to her family? Have you finished with her services?'

'Yes, it is better for everyone.'

'But this breaks our agreement. You promised not to make any changes, but to continue living as you had before, to protect Sir Leicester.

'My Lady, it is well known that you like this girl. This action will cause people to talk, and any doubts about you or how Chesney Wold is run cannot be good for Sir Leicester. Your secret is now *my* secret, and *I* will decide how to use it to protect Sir Leicester and the family.'

They are silent for a few minutes. Finally Lady Dedlock says, 'Is it your plan to tell Sir Leicester my history tonight?'

'No, not tonight,' the lawyer says with a confident smile. 'It may be tomorrow, but I won't say anything more. Good night. I am going home.'

Lady Dedlock cannot rest. She looks out at the moon and decides to walk alone in a garden which is for the use of the owners of surrounding houses. A servant opens the gate for her and gives her the key. She will return when she has cleared her aching head.

What is that? Who fired a gun? Where was it?

People stop and look around. A few windows and doors are opened, and some people come outside. The dogs and cats make a lot of noise, but the excitement soon ends. Before ten o'clock the streets are quiet again.

Early the next morning a servant enters Mr Tulkinghorn's office, screams and runs out again. Soon there is an anxious crowd in the street wanting to find out what has happened. The police arrive and examine every corner of Mr Tulkinghorn's rooms. Why? Because the lawyer's time on this earth has ended; he has been shot through the heart.

◆

George Rouncewell's plans for this fine day include visiting his friends, the Bagnets, to celebrate Mrs Bagnet's birthday. He is enjoying the company of the family when a knock is heard at the door.

'George,' says the man, 'how have you been?'

'It is Bucket!' cries George.

'Yes,' says the man, coming in and closing the door. 'I am sorry to interrupt this lovely party, but I have some urgent business with Mr Rouncewell. I wonder if you could come with me, George?'

'Happy Birthday to you, Mrs Bagnet, and I will say goodbye to all of you,' says George as the two men leave the house.

'Now George, old boy,' says Bucket, 'it is my duty to tell you that you are in police **custody** for the murder of Tulkinghorn, the lawyer. Be careful what you say now. Can you prove where you were last night at ten o'clock?'

'Last night? Last night? Well, yes, I was there last night!'

'Yes, and I also know that you have been to Mr Tulkinghorn's rooms often recently, and you have been heard arguing and shouting at him, and he has been heard calling you a dangerous type. I have no choice, George; I must take you to the police station and hold you there. It's my duty.'

'Your duty is to **arrest** an innocent man? But I suppose the law will find a way to make me guilty,' George says angrily.

'George, it is better if you say nothing without a lawyer,' advises Bucket.

'A lawyer? I wouldn't have anything to do with one of *them*. They bring trouble. I am innocent. And I was not the only person at Tulkinghorn's last night. Do you already know that?'

'George, can you help me with this case and help yourself, too?'

'It is true that I hated Tulkinghorn, and I went to his office last night. As I was going up the stairs, I saw another person coming down. It was dark, but

custody /ˈkʌstədi/ (n) the state of being kept in prison until you appear in court, because the police believe that you are responsible for a crime

arrest /əˈrest/ (v/n) to be taken away by a police officer because you are believed to be guilty of a crime

I could see that it was a lady wearing a long black coat with a deep **fringe** on it. I almost spoke to her because just for a second I thought it was Miss Summerson from Bleak House. But I watched her from the window and saw that, although she looked something like Miss Summerson, it was not her.'

'That proves nothing, George, but it might help me. Unfortunately, we know that *you* were there last night, and you are going to prison now.'

Mr Bucket leaves George Rouncewell in prison, but continues his search for the murderer. He spends every hour watching, listening, asking questions and collecting information. His home for the moment is with the Dedlocks. Sir Leicester has said, 'Mr Bucket, I want you to solve this crime. Do everything you can – I will pay your bill, every penny. I cannot believe that my friend, my lawyer, has been murdered. The whole matter has upset me greatly. I worry that I may never be the same again.'

After Mr Tulkinghorn's burial service, Bucket is interrupted by a servant: 'Here's another letter for you, Mr Bucket. It arrived by post.'

'Another one?' says Mr Bucket. He knows that letters can be dangerous things. He has received six of them in the last twenty-four hours. They all say the same thing: 'LADY DEDLOCK'.

Mr Bucket does not discuss the letters with Sir Leicester or with anyone else for the moment. Instead, he follows his own methods.

'Sir Leicester,' Mr Bucket begins at the end of this difficult day, 'may I make an appointment to meet with you tomorrow morning? I shall discover the few things that I need to complete the case before then.'

'I will see you then,' replies Sir Leicester.

Mr Bucket stops in front of the fireplace in the hall to have a conversation with a servant positioned there. After exchanging a few pleasant words, Bucket asks, 'Is My Lady out for the evening?'

'Yes, sir, out to dinner,' answers the servant. 'She's out most days.'

Suddenly the doors open and Lady Dedlock passes through the hall.

'Mr Bucket,' she says, 'are you waiting to see me? Have you discovered anything more about the murder?'

'Nothing to discuss at the moment, My Lady.'

Lady Dedlock disappears up the stairs and Bucket turns to the servant and says, 'She is a lovely lady, but she doesn't look quite healthy.'

'You're right there,' says the servant. 'She suffers from headaches.'

'Walking is good for headaches,' suggests Bucket. 'Didn't Lady Dedlock go out for a walk on the night of this business with Mr Tulkinghorn? I think I saw

---

fringe /frɪndʒ/ (n) a decoration on a curtain or piece of clothing, which is made of thin hanging strings along the edge

her going into the neighbouring garden at about ten o'clock. She was wearing a long black coat with a deep fringe, wasn't she?'

'That's right, but it was half-past nine when I unlocked the garden and left her there with the key.'

After breakfast the next morning, Mr Bucket meets Sir Leicester in the library, and goes straight to his main point. 'Sir Leicester, I now have the facts that I need to name the person who did this crime.'

'Is it the soldier, Mr Rouncewell?' asks Sir Leicester.

'No, Sir Leicester, not the soldier. It was a woman.'

Sir Leicester is shocked.

'Sir, it is my duty to tell you some things that will upset you, but I promise that your family's secrets are safe with me. May I begin by saying that everyone admires Lady Dedlock. She is a model of the finest behaviour.'

'Sir, I must ask you to leave my wife out of this conversation.'

'I am afraid that is impossible, Sir Leicester,' explains Bucket. 'She is at the centre of everything that has happened.'

'Officer, you know your duty, but be very careful how you use My Lady's name. I will not allow you to hurt her or to damage her name.'

'Sir Leicester, I shall say what I must say, and nothing more.'

And then Mr Bucket tells Sir Leicester everything he knows about Lady Dedlock's past: her relationship with Captain Hawdon, the baby that she thought was dead, Captain Hawdon's death and the love letters that he left behind – and Miss Esther Summerson. He explains how Tulkinghorn was using this information against Lady Dedlock, and that she went to the lawyer's rooms on the night of his murder.

Sir Leicester covers his face with his hands, and when he looks up again, he finds it difficult to speak. The words will not form themselves correctly on his tongue. But finally he asks: 'Why? Why did Mr Tulkinghorn say nothing of this to me?'

'Sir Leicester, I advise you to speak to your wife. She can explain. I have the letters to Captain Hawdon which I found in Tulkinghorn's office, and I will not show them to anyone else.'

'But will the murderer be arrested soon?' asks Sir Leicester.

'That person is now in this house,' continues Bucket. 'I plan to take her into custody here, with you present. Please follow my directions. Don't say a word, and agree with me when I look towards you.'

Mr Bucket rings the bell and a servant brings the Frenchwoman, Miss Hortense, into the room. She turns very pale when she sees the detective.

'Sir Leicester, Miss Hortense used to work for Lady Dedlock as her maid. She has been renting the extra bedroom at my house for some weeks.'

'Why is this of interest to Sir Leicester Dedlock?' demands the Frenchwoman. 'And why has Mrs Bucket brought me here? I do not want to be part of your foolish games. I will leave this minute!'

'Now, miss, you stay quiet and sit on the sofa.'

'I will not sit down on any sofa!' Hortense shouts. 'Why should I?'

'Because I am taking you into custody for the murder of Mr Tulkinghorn. I can speak to you politely, while you sit on the sofa, or I can speak to you roughly while we travel to the police station. It is your choice.'

She sits down, saying, 'You are an animal!'

'Quiet! Now, Sir Leicester, this young woman worked for Lady Dedlock until your wife asked her to leave.'

'That was my decision!' shouts Hortense. 'I wish for trouble, only trouble, for this house and everyone in it.'

'Miss, behave yourself,' continues Bucket. 'Sir Leicester, this woman also had a complaint against Mr Tulkinghorn after she did a little job for him, for which she was well paid.'

'I threw his money at him!'

'This won't help you, miss. Since this young woman has been renting a room in my house, with the probable aim of watching me at work, she has had a habit of visiting the lawyer's house and annoying him.

'On the day after the murder, I arrested George Rouncewell – he hated Tulkinghorn and had been seen at his house on that terrible night. But I didn't believe that Rouncewell was the murderer.

'I went home that night and watched Miss Hortense closely. She was being too friendly, too nice to my wife. Then, when I saw her pick up a knife from the table, I suddenly realised that she was the murderer. But she had been to the theatre the night before, and had been seen at the beginning of the play and at the end. The murder happened between those times.

'My wife helped me to get more facts about Miss Hortense. She saw her writing those letters to me, and she wrote one to you, too. Here it is. It says: LADY DEDLOCK MURDERER. Miss Hortense wanted to blame Lady Dedlock for the murder.'

'Lies!' shouts the Frenchwoman. 'It is all lies!'

'But I wanted to find the gun, and with my wife's help, I did. Miss Hortense invited Mrs Bucket to go to a pretty little café near a small stream in the countryside. At tea, this young woman excused herself for some minutes, and when she returned to the table she was breathing heavily. A few hours later my men found the gun at the bottom of the stream. The case is closed. We have the murderer.'

'Animal! I would like to kill you – and your wife, too! And this old man – can you make him better? He is like a child now. And can you make his wife's disgrace disappear? No! Do with me as you want. It is only death.' She turned to Sir Leicester. 'Goodbye, old man. I hate you and I pity you!'

After Mr Bucket leaves with Hortense, Sir Leicester is alone. He is sad and confused and his body is broken. He thinks about his wife and his love for her, which nothing can change, and then he falls to the floor.

CHAPTER 10

Esther's Story: A Hopeless Search

I went to St Albans to see the dear one once more – only to see her, not to speak to her or let her know that I was near. I also wanted to be lost.

Mr Jarndyce, Ada and I were in London again to celebrate Ada's twenty-first birthday. Mr Jarndyce invited Mr Allan Woodcourt to join our party to mark the fact that Ada was now an adult and could make her own decisions.

Before our trip to London, I felt that Ada was not her usual cheerful self, and, not wanting to keep any secrets from her, I decided to tell her that I was going to become Mr Jarndyce's wife and the lady of Bleak House. She was so pleased and happy for me that I became ten times happier than I had been before, and as we left for London, I felt that everything was as it should be.

The birthday dinner was very pleasant, but I know that the four of us felt sad because Richard was absent from our table. After that day Ada and I saw less of each other than usual because I was helping a sick friend. Mr Woodcourt was this friend's doctor, so I saw him quite often during those weeks. He was so gentle and skilful with his patient that I admired him more than ever. He was also helping Mr Badger in his medical practice, but he had not yet found a position with good pay for himself.

When my friend was better and I had more time at home, I began to notice a change in my dear Ada. I saw signs of worry and sadness on her face. I wondered if she was unhappy about the idea of my marriage to Mr Jarndyce and the changes that this would bring to Bleak House. Sometimes I was certain that Ada wanted to tell me something, but she always stopped herself.

One morning I suggested that Ada and I should visit Richard. It surprised me that she did not agree immediately.

'Ada, have you and Richard argued?'

'No, Esther, there is nothing wrong between us.' But I could see tears in her eyes as she said these words.

Soon we were out of the house and looking for Richard's rooms, which I knew were near the Court of Chancery, very near his lawyer's office. I had never been there before and was surprised when Ada found the place with no trouble. We were soon at his door and Ada entered without knocking.

'Ada! Esther! How wonderful to see you,' he said. 'You have just missed Woodcourt – he is the best friend that a man could have, and visits me often.'

'He has kept his promise to me,' I thought to myself.

There were books and papers everywhere, and many had the words Jarndyce and Jarndyce on them. I also noticed that Richard's eyes appeared large and sunken, his lips looked dry, and his body was very thin.

'Do you think this is a healthy place to live, Richard?' I asked.

'It is all right for now, but I will leave here in one of two ways soon. Either there will be an end to our suit, or an end to the suitor. But it will be the suit – don't worry about that! My lawyer and I are doing very well. We understand the case,' he said confidently, but he looked hungry and worried. 'You two remind me of the old days when we three were together and so happy. Sometimes I miss those happy days ... I get so tired!'

Ada went to him and put her arms around his neck. 'Esther, dear,' she said very quietly, 'I am not going home again. I am going to stay here with my dear husband. We have been married for two months.'

I held Ada in my arms. I loved her and Richard very, very much, but I felt pity for them at that moment.

'Please forgive us,' Ada cried. 'When I reached twenty-one, we quietly got married. I wanted to tell you, but I worried that you would be in a difficult position if we asked you to keep the news from my cousin John.'

'I have nothing to forgive,' I said. I pitied them, but did not want to damage their happiness. 'I will leave you now, but I must warn you that I won't stay away. I will visit you tomorrow and as often as I can.'

After several goodbyes, I was outside alone and then I cried. I felt so lonely and lost without Ada beside me. What would happen to my two dear friends in that awful place, with Richard worrying about Jarndyce and Jarndyce and going slowly mad?

My guardian had come home after visiting the poor boy I had found at St Albans. The boy was dead, but I did not know it. When I entered the house Mr Jarndyce said, 'You have been crying, little woman.'

'Yes, Ada is not with me, and is so very sorry, Guardian.'

'Is she married, my dear?' Mr Jarndyce asked.

I told him the story, and how Ada hoped that he would forgive her.

'There is no need,' he said. 'But our house is quickly growing very thin.'

'But *I* will not leave you, and I will do everything I can to make Bleak House a happy place.'

'And you will be successful in that,' said Mr Jarndyce. He put his hand on mine and turned his bright, fatherly look on me.

I felt sad that this was all we could say. I worried that I had not done or said more since the letter and my answer.

◆

I was asleep when my guardian knocked very loudly on my bedroom door at about one o'clock, and told me to get up immediately. In a great rush he said that my mother had run away, and that there was now a person at our door who was searching for her under orders from Sir Leicester Dedlock. This man, a detective named Mr Bucket, believed that my mother would be less frightened when he found her if I was with him. I was so nervous and upset that I did not understand the situation clearly, but I knew that my mother was in trouble and that I must try to help her.

I put on my warmest clothes and hurried downstairs. Mr Bucket, in a low voice, read a letter to me that my mother had left for Sir Leicester, and within minutes I was sitting beside him in the waiting carriage.

As we began our search of the streets of London, Mr Bucket asked politely about my handkerchief, which he had found in my mother's drawer. I explained about the brick-makers near St Albans and about Jenny's dead baby, and about a lady in a veil who had paid her for the handkerchief. With this information, Mr Bucket seemed able to form a plan.

First we went to the police station and Mr Bucket left a description of Lady Dedlock with the officers on duty. Then we headed for the river, where a body had been found – fortunately, it was not my mother. Then we stopped at late pubs and travellers' hotels, and at each place Mr Bucket jumped quickly out of the carriage, went inside and then hurried back, shouting, 'Continue, driver!' After examining the empty streets of London, we left the houses behind and were on the dark, snow-covered road towards St Albans.

'Have you found out anything about Lady Dedlock, Mr Bucket?' I asked.

'Nothing certain yet, but we haven't lost much time. Don't worry.'

With more stops and more questions along the way, it was between five and six o'clock when we arrived at a travellers' resting place a few kilometres from Bleak House. Mr Bucket hurried inside and came back with a hot cup of tea for me. I thanked him and asked about our progress.

'It is all right, miss. She has been seen. I think we are on the right road. She passed through here yesterday evening at about nine o'clock.' Then he took my cup and shouted, 'Continue, driver!' There was no time to lose.

We stopped at Bleak House to see if anyone had been there asking for me or Mr Jarndyce, but no one had come to the door in the last twenty-four hours.

'Now, Miss Summerson,' said Mr Bucket, 'we shall hurry to the brick-makers' houses. You will ask the questions since they have met you before.'

We found Jenny's husband and her friend Liz and her husband at the table eating breakfast in Jenny's poor little house. They recognised me and Liz invited me to sit down. Mr Bucket stood quietly beside the fireplace.

'Liz,' I said, 'we have come a long way in the night to find a lady.'

'A lady who was here last night,' added Mr Bucket.

I knew that Liz would talk to me if she were alone, but she was frightened of her husband, who was often violent.

'I would like to see Jenny very much,' I said quietly. 'I think she could help us to find this lady. Will she be here soon?'

Liz started to answer, but her husband kicked her under the table with his heavy boot. Jenny's husband looked up and said, 'I don't like you rich people coming to my house like you owned it. What would you do if I arrived at your door? But you're not as bad as some of them, so I'll tell you. Jenny won't be here soon; she went to London. Last night.'

'But was Jenny here when the lady came? Did they talk to each other?' I asked. 'We are very worried about this lady. Can you help us at all?'

After a long silence, Jenny's husband said, 'She was here and they talked. She was looking for the young lady from up at the big house – she gave Jenny a handkerchief when the last baby died, and this lady had given us money for the handkerchief. Jenny said the young ladies weren't there, at the big house. Then the lady asked if she could rest for a few minutes beside our fire. At about midnight she went one way and Jenny went another, towards London.'

I looked at Liz's husband and asked him if I could ask his wife a question.

'Ask then, but keep it short!' he shouted.

'Liz, how did the lady look? Did she speak much?' I asked.

'She looked very pale, very bad. Her clothes and shoes were wet, and she was very tired. We gave her a little tea and bread but she ate very little.'

'And when she left here ... ' I was trying to ask more questions, but Jenny's husband interrupted me.

'When she left here, she was travelling north on the high road. Now we're finished with you,' he said.

When we were outside again, Mr Bucket said, 'There is something that they are not telling us. You could see that the woman had more to tell, but her husband didn't allow her to speak. It is possible that this Jenny went to London with a message for you, and it is possible that Lady Dedlock paid her husband for that job, and for keeping quiet about it.'

We changed horses again at Bleak House and continued our journey. I became more and more nervous because our progress through the heavy snow was very slow. Mr Bucket was up and down at every house, asking questions, shaking hands, having a quick drink. But he never seemed to waste a minute, and then shouted, 'Continue, driver!'

After each stop, Mr Bucket reported to me, 'Don't worry, miss. She has been here. They have seen a lady in her dress, travelling on foot.'

The snow continued through the day and a fog came down early, so we were travelling in very cold, wet, dark conditions. After more stops and more

questions, I could see that Mr Bucket was less confident than he had been. At last, when we were changing horses again, he told me that he had lost sight of the dress. He was not worried yet, thinking that he would find it again at the next stop, but no one had seen a lady in the dress we were looking for. Night was coming again and my mother's path had disappeared.

We stopped at a large hotel, warmed ourselves at a big fire and had a little soup and bread. Mr Bucket had a few words with the people at the hotel, and then he returned to me. He looked quite excited.

'What is it? Is she here?' I asked anxiously.

'No, no. Nobody is here. But I have realised! We have been following the wrong dress. We are going back to London.' And within minutes we were in the carriage and our new horses were racing towards that city.

It was three o'clock in the morning when the countryside disappeared and we began to pass city houses. We had been on the road for more than twenty-four hours, but Mr Bucket's energy never failed him, and I was confident that he knew what he was doing.

Before four o'clock we were in a much smaller carriage and were travelling along the narrowest and worst streets in London. Mr Bucket stopped often and questioned the local police officers. Finally he came back to the carriage and asked if I was able to get out and walk a short distance. Of course, I got out immediately and took his arm. We were near Chancery Lane and I heard the clocks strike half-past five.

We turned a very narrow corner and I heard someone shout my name. I knew the voice very well. It was Mr Woodcourt.

'My dear Miss Summerson, I have just come from Richard and Ada's house – don't worry, they are as well as we can expect. But should you be out at this hour and in such weather?' He took off his coat and put it around my shoulders. 'May I go with you? Mr Jarndyce has told me something about this business.'

Now the three of us turned into a narrower street and stopped at Snagsby's Office Materials, Law-Writing and Copying shop. A police officer had noticed a woman going to that door late last night. Mr Bucket knocked on the door and soon the three of us and the police officer were inside.

'Mr Snagsby, we have information about a lady who came here, we believe, late last night. Did you have a visitor after closing time?' asked Mr Bucket.

'I am sorry, sir, but I closed the shop and didn't see any new customers after that,' reported Mr Snagsby.

'But do you have a servant, Mr Snagsby?'

'Yes, sir. Guster, quite a nervous girl, works for us in the house.'

'Will you bring her in here as quickly as you can,' said Bucket.

Guster entered the room, looking very worried, but soon she was answering Mr Bucket's questions.

'I was delivering something for Mr Snagsby long after it was dark. When I came home I found a poor-looking woman staring at our house. She was all wet and muddy and she said she'd lost her way. She was so tired and pale that you had to feel sorry for her. But she sounded like a lady. And then she asked where the burial ground for poor people was – the one with a step and a big iron gate that was always locked. She meant the place where they put Mr Nemo – you remember him, don't you, Mr Snagsby?'

I could see that Mr Snagsby did remember, and Mr Bucket began to look very anxious.

'She asked me how to find the place and I told her. Before she left, she gave me this letter to send. It has the address on it, but she didn't have any money for the post. I told her I knew what it was like to be poor and promised to send it for her. She thanked me and then she went.'

The letter was addressed to me and Mr Bucket asked me to read it to him. I could see that different parts had been written at different times. I read what follows:

I went to St Albans to see the dear one once more – only to see her, not to speak to her or let her know that I was near. I also wanted to be lost. I gave the brick-maker my watch so he would let his wife help me.

The next part, written later, said: *I have walked for many hours and I know that I will soon die. These streets! I am cold, wet and tired, and this condition could cause my death, but I shall die from terror and disgrace.*

'Be brave!' Mr Bucket said to me. 'There are only a few more words. They were probably written even later, perhaps in the dark.'

I have done all that I could to be lost. I shall soon be forgotten, so I hope that I will disgrace him less. I will leave this letter now with this kind maid. If I can get so far, I will lie down at the place that has been often in my mind, near him. Goodbye. Forgive.

'My dear, don't think that I have a hard heart, but when you can, we should follow her to the burial ground,' said Mr Bucket.

'Mr Woodcourt, please don't leave me now,' I said.

At last we stood on a dark street, and at the end we could see the locked iron gate with the burial ground on the other side. It was a horrible spot, surrounded by poor, dirty houses with a few dull lights in the windows. I noticed a body lying on the wet step at the gate – it was Jenny, the mother of the dead child.

I ran forwards, but Mr Bucket and Mr Woodcourt stopped me.

'Miss Summerson,' Mr Bucket said very gently, 'you will understand me if you think for a moment. They changed clothes at the brick-maker's house. One walked towards London and one went towards the north and then went home. Think for a moment!'

I did not understand. Mr Bucket and Mr Woodcourt stood silently and looked at me. Then Mr Bucket said to Mr Woodcourt, 'She had better go. Her hands should be the first to touch her.'

I moved to the gate and bent down. I lifted the head, moved the long wet hair away from the face. And it was my mother, cold and dead.

6.1 Were you right?

Look back at your answers to Activity 5.4. Then decide whose words these might be.

1 'I would do anything to help my dear, dear husband.' ....

2 'I will not rest until the murderer is in police custody.' ....

3 'You'll do exactly as I say or face disaster.' ....

4 'I know Richard blames me, but I want to help him.' ....

5 'Do not connect my wife's name with anything unpleasant.'. ....

6 'I prefer dry land to a sinking ship.' ....

7 'How can I help Ada and Richard in their poor flat?' ....

8 'I'm not a good husband yet, but one day ...' ....

9 'My lies will destroy my husband and his family.' ....

6.2 What more did you learn?

Complete Mr Bucket's reports. Write the full reports in your notebook.

1
Death of Mr Tulkinghorn
Time: ....
Place: ....
Method: ....
Possible murderers: ....

....

Information about Miss
Hortense that helped solve the
crime:
1) Mrs Bucket saw her writing
letters that said: ....

....

2) She was not in her seat at
the .... when the murder
happened.
3) She threw a .... into
a stream in the countryside.

2
Search for Lady Dedlock
Late at night: Found ....
.... and searched the streets
of .... with her, then went
towards the town of ....
.... Brick-makers said
the lady went .... on the
high road; Jenny went towards
....
Realised we were following the
wrong .... Turned south.
5.30 in the morning: Met up with
Mr .... near .... Lane.
..........., Snagsby's servant, had
a .... from Lady Dedlock
and gave her directions to the
.... for the poor.
Found her body there.

6.3 **Language in use**

Look at the sentences on the right.
Then complete these sentences with
a name and the correct form of a
verb from the boxes below.

> Sir Leicester, I **advise you to speak** to
> your wife.
>
> You could see that the woman had
> more to tell, but her husband **didn't**
> **allow her to speak**.

Mr Bucket   Mr Woodcourt Lady Dedlock
Miss Hortense   George Rouncewell

send   be   discover
celebrate   help

1 Mr Tulkinghorn doesn't want ....
  Rosa back to her family.

2 Mr Bucket asks .... him find the
  murderer.

3 His wife helps .... more facts
  about the Frenchwoman, Miss Hortense.

4 Mr Jarndyce invites .... Ada's
  birthday with him and Esther.

5 Mr Bucket orders .... quiet while
  he tells Sir Leicester about the murder.

6.4 **What happens next?**

What will you find out in Chapters 11 and 12? Underline one of the possible
endings to each sentence.

1 George Rouncewell *stays in prison for several years / is out of prison in a few days.*

2 Sir Leicester is looked after in his old age by *Mrs Rouncewell and her son George /
  Ada and Mr Jarndyce.*

3 Lady Dedlock is buried *at Chesney Wold / beside Captain Hawdon.*

4 Esther Summerson marries *Mr John Jarndyce / Mr Allan Woodcourt.*

5 When the case of Jarndyce and Jarndyce comes to an end, Richard and Ada
  become very rich / get nothing.

6 Another person dies before the end of the story: *Richard Carstone / Mr John
  Jarndyce.*

CHAPTER 11

Back Home

*'If that happens, remember to say to Lady Honoria, and to the world,
that my love for my wife has never changed and will never change.'*

So what happened to make Lady Dedlock finally leave her loving husband and comfortable home, and abandon her place in society?

While Sir Leicester was lying forgotten on the floor of his library, in another part of the Dedlocks' London house My Lady was talking to Mrs Rouncewell, the housekeeper from Chesney Wold.

'Mrs Rouncewell,' said Lady Dedlock in surprise, 'what are you doing in London? Has something happened? What is the matter? Tell me, please.'

'Trouble, My Lady. Sad trouble. Friends of my younger son sent for me and I came immediately,' Mrs Rouncewell explained. 'I have seen George after all these years – he is in custody for the murder of Mr Tulkinghorn. My Lady, I have a letter that was delivered to me last night at Chesney Wold. I have not spoken of it to anyone. Please read it after I have gone; then, if you pity him, please help him. Without a doubt, my son is innocent.'

After the housekeeper left, Lady Dedlock opened the letter and saw a newspaper report of the death of Mr Tulkinghorn. At the bottom of the page was her own name with the word MURDERER written beside it.

Then, without warning, a servant told My Lady that Mr Guppy was at the door and wished to speak to her.

Mr Guppy had a short message: 'Madam, Captain Hawdon's packet of letters was not burned with Mr Krook, but was found in Tulkinghorn's office after his death. The letters will not stay secret for much longer.'

Alone, Lady Dedlock knew that she would never escape her past, even with Mr Tulkinghorn dead. In a rush she wrote this letter to her husband and left it on her table before hurrying out of the house:

Please believe me: I am innocent of the murder of Mr Tulkinghorn. I am guilty of everything else that people will tell you. Tulkinghorn said that he would tell you everything, so I followed him on the night of his murder. I wanted to stop him from ruining our life together. I found his house dark and silent. I rang twice at his door, but there was no reply and I came home.

Please forget me. I am afraid that you have wasted your love and care on me. I am leaving so my past does not bring disgrace on you and your family. This is my final goodbye to you.

She dressed quickly, covered her head with her veil and left all her jewels and money behind. She listened, went downstairs when the hall was empty, opened and shut the great door and escaped into the cold wind.

◆

Much later, after knocking softly,
a servant entered the library and
found Sir Leicester lying on the floor,
looking like a dead man.

The servant rang the bell, a doctor
was sent for, but no one could find
Lady Dedlock. Her letter to her
husband was found on her table, but
Sir Leicester, although not dead, was
unable to speak or to open a letter. He
was now a sick old man, lying on his
bed, fighting to stay alive.

When he opened his eyes,
Sir Leicester was glad to see Mrs
Rouncewell at his bedside, but he
still could not speak. Finally his old
housekeeper brought him paper and a
pencil. He wrote: 'My Lady.'

'My Lady went out before you
became ill, sir, and she doesn't know
of your illness yet,' Mrs Rouncewell explained.

This news upset him greatly, and Mrs Rouncewell gave him the letter that
Lady Dedlock had left for him. He read it with tears in his eyes, and the doctor
feared that he was getting worse again. Finally he wrote 'Mr B' on his piece of
paper, and Mr Bucket, who had returned from the police station, hurried into
the room. Sir Leicester put his wife's letter in the detective's hand and wrote on
his paper: 'I forgive everything. Find ... ' Mr Bucket stopped his hand.

'Sir Leicester Dedlock, I shall find her. Not a minute to lose.'

As he was leaving to begin his hopeful, but in the end hopeless search for
Lady Dedlock, Mr Bucket had a quick word with Mrs Rouncewell. 'Your son
George is as innocent as you are, he is out of prison and he will visit you today.
Now, before I leave, may I have a quick look at Lady Dedlock's rooms? There
might be something there that could help me find her.'

My Lady's rooms were in perfect order and everything was of the highest
quality, but Mr Bucket noticed something that did not fit with the other things.
It was a handkerchief, and it had a mark on it. 'Esther Summerson,' Bucket said
to himself. 'Come with me – I'll take *you*.'

He went straight to Mr Jarndyce's London apartment.

'Mr John Jarndyce, please do not be worried by this visit. Lady Dedlock has disappeared and Sir Leicester has asked me to find her. He is in a terrible state and we must not waste a minute.'

Mr Jarndyce read Lady Dedlock's letter quickly.

'The lady doesn't want to bring disgrace to Sir Leicester, and she believes that people think she murdered Mr Tulkinghorn,' continued Mr Bucket. 'If Miss Summerson is with me, she will know that we have come as friends. But now time flies; it is almost one o'clock and she will be further from here.'

Mr Jarndyce went to Esther Summerson's room and soon returned with her. That was when the search began.

◆

Sir Leicester Dedlock continued to be very ill, and could do nothing to help in the search for his wife. But when the sun came up, he had his bed moved closer to the window, hoping to see her return.

Mrs Rouncewell had the help of her dear son George, who had arrived at the house the night before. They had a good long talk, and the old soldier was doing everything possible to help his mother and Sir Leicester.

'George, I have been with this family for almost sixty years, but I am afraid it is being destroyed,' Mrs Rouncewell said at breakfast. 'I am thankful to have lived long enough to see you, and to be here to help Sir Leicester, but who will tell him if something happens to My Lady? Who will tell him!'

In Sir Leicester's room, a servant asked Mrs Rouncewell about her son.

Sir Leicester looked at Mrs Rouncewell with a question in his eyes.

'Sir, I have found George. He has come home.'

Sir Leicester worked hard to get his words out: 'Bring George to me!'

There was a happy meeting between the old soldier and Sir Leicester. Many apologies from George, many smiles from the sick old man.

'My boy, can I tell you something?' Sir Leicester said slowly, and with great difficulty. 'My wife has gone on a journey; we have had a difference of opinion, but not an argument. Can I say something with you and your mother as my witnesses? Perhaps I will become worse; perhaps I will die. If that happens, remember to say to Lady Honoria, and to the world, that my love for my wife has never changed and *will* never change. She is everything to me.'

◆

Lady Dedlock's body is brought back to Chesney Wold, but the fashionable world doesn't know how she died. Sir Leicester, with George Rouncewell at his

side, visits her burial place almost every day. The old man is not strong and is almost blind, but George protects him and is good company for him.

George can be seen each Sunday morning at church with his dear old mother, and the two of them often visit Mrs Rouncewell's older son and his family farther north. The two brothers are great friends again, and the older brother's children love their Uncle George.

And what about Chesney Wold? Sir Leicester's home is very different from the exciting days when the beautiful Lady Honoria Dedlock governed it like a queen. Many of the rooms are dark now, and few visitors come through the gates. To the stranger's eye, it seems a very dull, sleepy place.

CHAPTER 12

Esther's Story: A New World

But my tears were not sad – they were happy. He had said he loved me, and that I would always be in his heart. His words had changed my life.

We stayed in London after my mother's death because I wanted to be close to Ada and Richard. I visited my dear friends daily in their little apartment near Chancery Lane. Their rooms were very poor, with little light and very little space, but Ada shone like a bright star in this hopeless corner of the city. She was a good wife and kept their home tidy and clean. She looked after Richard and was always careful to stay away from the subject of Jarndyce and Jarndyce.

But when Richard was at home it was impossible to escape from the suit in Chancery. It was the only thing on his mind, and he was either at the court – usually with mad Miss Flite – or working on Jarndyce and Jarndyce at his table in the apartment. His health was ruined, and although he was always happy to see me, he could never stay cheerful for very long.

Mr Allan Woodcourt was also often at Ada and Richard's house. He had kept his promise to me and was the best friend that Richard had in those days. He advised him as a doctor, but more than anything, he reminded him that there was life outside the court, with fresh air, laughter, music.

I was always pleased to see Mr Woodcourt, and I learned that he had been offered a position in a medical practice in the north of England, and that he would move there in about six months' time. He would not make a fortune, but he would be of great use to many people.

One day when I had joined Ada and Richard for supper, Mr Woodcourt came in after we had eaten and invited Richard to go for a walk on one of the bridges and enjoy the airy night. I was happy to be left alone with Ada.

'My dearest, Richard is always happiest when he is with Mr Woodcourt. We must thank *you* for that. And now, can you help me in another way?'

'Ada, I would do anything for you!' I cried.

'I want to be a good wife. Can you teach me? When I married Richard, I thought that if we were together, he would give up Jarndyce and Jarndyce and try to make a good life for us – but he cannot give it up. I never talk about the case in Chancery, but I see Richard worrying about it day and night. I try to love him and help him in my small way.'

I held Ada's hand and felt certain that she had something important that she urgently wanted to tell me.

'But there is something that helps me to stay strong, Esther. Something that gives me hope. I am going to have a baby, and I hope that Richard will give up Jarndyce and Jarndyce and try to make his son or daughter proud of him. This hope keeps me strong, but there are times when I am full of fear.'

'What causes that, dear Ada?' I asked gently.

'I fear that Richard will not live to see his child.'

◆

The months passed and I was at Richard and Ada's little apartment as often as possible. One evening Mr Allan Woodcourt offered to walk back to Mr Jarndyce's house with me because it was very late. We talked about Richard and Ada and their difficult situation, and I thanked him again for all the help he gave them.

We were standing outside Mr Jarndyce's house when I learned that Mr Woodcourt's heart was full of true, generous, unshakeable love for me. Oh, too late to know it now, too late, too late.

'Esther, when I came back from my foreign travels,' Mr Woodcourt said, 'I learned how ill you had been, but I found the same sweet, wonderful young woman, always kind, always free from selfish thoughts. I loved you more then than before, and I love you more each day.'

'Mr Woodcourt, I do not deserve your love and I am not free to accept it,' I said sadly. My heart was breaking, but I was certain that my life would be better knowing that he loved me. I would do my best to deserve his love.

'Esther, I have wanted to say these words to you for a very long time, but

I came home as poor as when I left. And now I learn that you are not free to accept my love. I won't upset you again with my feelings, but I will keep you in my heart, and I hope that we will continue as friends.'

'Mr Woodcourt, your words are the most valuable words ever spoken to me. While I live, I will never forget the happiness of being loved by you. But I must say one more thing before you go. There has been one person since my childhood who has given me everything. He is the most generous, most unselfish, most loving person in the world.'

'I agree with your opinion,' he replied. 'You are speaking of Mr Jarndyce.'

'Very few people understand how good his character is, but I see it every day, and I am happy to share a future with him. I hope you can be happy for me, and for him,' I said, trying to be brave.

When Mr Woodcourt was gone, I stood at my dark window and looked out at the street. My strength of mind failed me and I cried. But my tears were not sad – they were happy. He had said that he loved me, and that I would always be in his heart. His words had changed my life.

Next morning I found my guardian in the Growlery and asked if I could have a private word. He looked very bright and happy, as usual.

'Guardian, have I acted as you wished since I brought the answer to your letter?' I asked.

'You have been everything that I could desire, dear Esther.'

'I am very glad to hear that,' I replied. 'Do you think we should talk about our future? I will be the lady of Bleak House when you wish.'

'Esther, I was thinking about the same subject this morning. Shall we give Bleak House its lady next month?' he said with a smile.

I agreed, and put my arms round his neck and kissed him.

We were interrupted by the arrival of Mr Bucket. He rushed into the room and shouted, 'Mr Jarndyce, Miss Summerson, I have exciting news. Another will in the case of Jarndyce and Jarndyce has been found!'

'But where was it found?' asked Mr Jarndyce.

'You remember Krook's property? It went into the hands of the Smallweeds, and little by little they looked through Krook's mountain of papers and the signature of Jarndyce caught old Smallweed's eye.

'He was so excited that he showed me the paper. I explained that, as a legal document, it didn't belong to Krook or to him, although I think he is expecting a reward. And here is the will itself. The paper is yellow and the edges are burned a little, but it is clearly a legal will.'

'Mr Bucket,' said my guardian, 'I haven't been interested in Jarndyce and Jarndyce for many years – my heart is sick of it – but we will speak to my lawyer and will ask him to advise the suitors.'

At the offices of Kenge and Carboy, Mr Kenge looked at the will and said, 'My dear sir, I believe this will is more recent than the others, and it has the necessary signatures and stamps; it is perfectly legal. When I present this document to the court next month, I hope that you will see that we are a great country, and that our legal **system** is a great system, Mr Jarndyce.'

'Sir,' replied Mr Jarndyce, 'do you ask *me* to believe that any good will come of Jarndyce and Jarndyce?'

'Wait and see, Mr Jarndyce, wait and see.'

◆

I prepared everything for my wedding quietly during the next weeks, because I was sure that my guardian would like it to be done this way. I also thought about Ada and the fact that she would be sorry to see my position at Bleak House change. My dear girl was always worried: she was expecting her baby soon, and Richard was in a very bad state. He had been excited about the new will and had studied it enthusiastically, but he was not strong enough to continue with any work for long. I secretly hoped that Richard and Ada would have good news about their suit before my marriage.

Because I was very busy, I was surprised when my guardian suggested a journey one morning. We were going to the north of England to see the place where Mr Allan Woodcourt would have his practice. Mr Jarndyce was in a very good mood and I began to wonder if he had done a great kindness to someone. After we had arrived at our hotel and had our dinner, he said, 'My dear, I have wanted to thank Mr Woodcourt for everything that he has done since we have known him. For helping poor Jo, for all his service to my two young cousins, and for his value to us all. When it was decided that he would move to this town, I looked for a little house for him, and I have found one. I have had it repaired, arranged the garden, bought some furniture. Now I want your opinion of it before I give it to him.'

My eyes filled with tears. My guardian was so kind, so good, so generous. I could not say a single word.

'Please don't cry, dear girl. This has already given me great pleasure.'

'This is wonderful, and my heart is full of thanks,' I said.

The next morning we went arm in arm to examine the house more closely, and I judged that it was perfect with its pretty rooms, beautiful garden and trees – all in a lovely area of the city. 'Guardian, it is wonderful!'

'And now, little woman,' said Mr Jarndyce, who looked very proud and happy, 'now, last of all, for the name of this house. Can you guess it?'

system /ˈsɪstəm/ (n) a group of connected parts that work together for a purpose

We went to the front of the house and he showed me, written over the door, the words BLEAK HOUSE. Then he took my hand and said, 'My dear, I want nothing more than your happiness. Now, listen to me and don't speak. When I sent you my letter, I believed that you and I could be happy together, but when Mr Woodcourt came home, I saw something else and I soon doubted my plan. I am your guardian and your father again. I know that you can find perfect happiness with Mr Woodcourt, and that is what I want for you.

'Don't cry again. I have looked forward to this day for months and months. I must explain that I talked to Allan Woodcourt before he spoke to you about his love. Afterwards he told me what you had said, and I have no more to say. Your future husband stood beside your father when he was dead; he stood beside your mother at the gate where she died. He has watched over all of us for a long time. Today I give Bleak House to its little lady and to him; and with God as my witness, this is the brightest day in all my life!'

◆

The time came for the newest will in Jarndyce and Jarndyce to be presented to the Court of Chancery, and although my guardian refused to go to the court, Allan and I wanted to support Richard. That morning we walked through the busy streets – so happily and strangely it seemed! – together. The area around the court was very crowded; we were fifteen minutes late and the day's business had begun, but many of the lawyers were laughing and heading for the door.

We asked a gentleman near us if he knew what was happening. He told us that Jarndyce and Jarndyce had ended.

'Ended for the day?' Allan asked.

'Ended forever!' the man shouted.

We stood to one side and watched as great piles and bags of papers were carried out of the courtroom. And everyone was shouting and laughing. Then we saw Mr Kenge and asked him to explain.

'The new will has not been looked at,' Kenge reported. 'After many years of study, knowledge, argument and intelligence, a decision has been reached: there will be no decision.'

'Mr Kenge,' said Allan, 'do I understand that all the money and property has gone for legal costs?'

'I believe so,' said Mr Kenge quietly. 'I am afraid that this is a sad day for English justice.'

'Dear Esther,' whispered Allan, 'this will break Richard's heart.'

'If you are looking for Mr Carstone, you will find him in the courtroom. He was resting there when I left,' said Mr Kenge.

Allan went to Richard. My guardian and I found them and Ada at the little apartment near the Court of Chancery a short time later.

'How is he?' was the first thing I said when Allan met us at the door.

'I found him sitting like a stone in the courtroom. He wanted to speak to the judge but his mouth began to fill with blood. Then I brought him here. He is very weak,' Allan told us. 'He has asked for you several times.'

Richard was lying on the sofa with his eyes closed when I went in. He looked very handsome, although his face was very pale. Ada sat at his side, holding his hand.

'My dear Esther,' he said when I sat beside his bed, 'give me a kiss.' His voice was weak but he had his old, attractive smile. He was happy for Allan and me, and promised to be at our wedding if he could stand on his feet.

It was not good for him to talk too much, and in the silence I knew. I knew!

He could not stay awake for long. He woke up when the door opened again and asked, 'Who is there?'

'Rick, it is me,' said Mr Jarndyce, and he placed his hand on Richard's.

'Oh, sir, cousin,' said Richard, 'you are a good man!' And he began to cry for the first time.

'My dear Rick, the clouds have cleared away and today is bright. We can see clearly now. And how are you, my dear boy?' asked Mr Jarndyce gently.

'I am very weak, sir, but I shall be stronger. I have to begin again in the world. I have learned a hard lesson, sir, but I will do better now.'

'Yes, yes, very well said!' cried my guardian.

'And I want to see the new Bleak House where Esther and Allan will live. Is that possible, sir? It will be like going to the old Bleak House again for the first time. Will you take Ada and me there, sir, and show it to us?'

'I certainly will,' replied Mr Jarndyce. 'I would like that very much.'

'Was it all a dream, sir? A troubled dream?'

'Nothing more, Rick. Nothing more,' Mr Jarndyce said.

'But I will begin again and make a new start! I will show my beautiful Ada how much she means to me, and I will prepare myself to be a guide to our child. When shall we go to the new Bleak House?' Richard asked hopefully.

'We will go soon, dear husband, very soon,' whispered Ada.

'Dear Ada, will you forgive me for all of the wrong I have done? Will you forgive me before I begin our new world?'

A smile lit up his face as Ada bent to kiss him. She held him in her arms, and with one painful cry he began again. Not in this world, but in the world without troubles, without pain, without worry.

◆

I have been the lady of Bleak House and the wife of Mr Allan Woodcourt for seven years now.

Richard and Ada's son was born within weeks of his father's death, and I, my husband and my guardian gave him his father's name. My dear Ada was a wonderful mother to her little baby. Again happy and full of hope, she moved back to the old Bleak House, but she, her pretty son and my guardian are often at the new Bleak House, and all the children – young Richard and my two little daughters – love both houses and their dear guardian.

Mr Jarndyce is a well-loved father to all of us, and he is my husband's best and dearest friend. I believe that he is happier than he has ever been, and Ada is not only happy, but certainly more beautiful and kinder than ever.

The bank would not say that we are rich, but we have everything we need. My husband is a great success in his profession, and we feel at home in this city and in our own Bleak House. Are we not rich?

On a recent evening, I was sitting outside looking at the moon when my husband came home.

'My dear wife, what are you doing out here?' asked Allan.

'I have been thinking,' I told him, 'about my past. I don't think that you could love me any better even if I had my old, prettier face.'

'My dear wife, do you ever look in a mirror?' Allan asked. 'Don't you know that you are prettier now than you have ever been?'

I did not know that, but I know that my dear children are very pretty, and that my friend Ada is beautiful, and that my husband is very handsome, and that my guardian has the brightest, kindest face in the world; and that they do not really need much beauty in me, even if I am ...

1 Six characters die in *Bleak House*: **Mr Nemo, Mr Krook, Mr Tulkinghorn, Jo, Lady Dedlock and Richard Carstone. Work with other students and discuss these questions, thinking about each character:**

a What caused his or her death?

b Was he or she responsible in any way for his or her own death?

c Which other people felt sad about the death of each of these characters? What was their relationship with the people who died?

d How were you affected by these deaths as readers of the story?

2 **Work with a partner. Choose one of the dead characters and decide on a scene that you can act out between that character and another character from the book.**

| **Student A** | You are the ghost of one of the dead characters. You are visiting someone from your past. Think about what you want to say to him or her before you speak. What questions do you want to ask? |

| **Student B** | You are the character who is visited by the ghost. Think about how you will answer the ghost's questions. How will you explain your actions since the ghost died? |

Prepare your scene and then act it out for the class. Try to entertain by making the scene funny, sad, romantic, mysterious or frightening.

1 **When he is much older, Mr John Jarndyce decides to write a book of his memories. Make notes, below, about the high points and low points in his relationship with these people and things.**

People in need: Mrs Jellyby, Miss Flite, young Jo
His wards: Esther Summerson, Ada Clare, Richard Carstone
The law: Jarndyce and Jarndyce, the Court of Chancery, suitors, lawyers, justice
Marriage: Lost dreams and happy endings

Notes

2 **Now choose one of the subjects and write, in your own notebook, a page of Mr Jarndyce's memories. Include reasons for him to feel happy and sad about the subject.**

1 In *Bleak House*, Charles Dickens writes about typical experiences that his characters, and people today, have during their lives. Discuss the lives of these four characters. How many good and bad experiences can you remember in their lives?

2 Write the words in the box on one of the lists below. Then work with a partner and add as many experiences as you can to each list.

romance	serious illness	regular job
birth of a child	car accident	destructive storm

GOOD EXPERIENCES

BAD EXPERIENCES

3 Read about one man's good and bad times.

Bad Times, .
Good Times

Mike Stanley, the drummer in the pop group The Mystery Men, lost one of his legs when he was a child. He remembers how he became a musician.

I was completely crazy about football. But my dreams of a profession in sport ended one day when I was hit by a lorry as I was walking home from school. For some time the doctors thought I was going to die.

I lived, but my right leg was broken so badly that it had to be cut off from the knee down. I was only ten then, and I was in and out of hospitals for years. I felt different from other children and spent a lot of time alone. I read a lot and even began to write poems. Then one day my dad gave me some of his old records from the 1960s, and for my fifteenth birthday he gave me some drums. I started writing music to go with my poems and found friends who could play the guitar and other instruments. We practised every evening and weekend, and finally our big chance came at the village hall one Saturday night.

We played two of the songs I had written and at the end the crowd went wild. At home I told my parents: 'You don't have to worry about me. I know what I'm going to do with my life.' That night was the beginning of a new, beautiful, confident life for me, and I've loved every minute of it.

4 Work in groups and discuss these questions.

a Do you admire Mike Stanley? Why (not)?

b Can you think of a real person or someone from a film or book who had a difficult but successful life? Tell the people in your group about that person.

5 **Work in groups of four. Prepare The Game of Chance.**

a   Look at your lists from Activity 2 and then write a good experience on each of the blue squares below. Write a bad experience on each pink square. Notice how far you can climb or fall from each square; this will help you to decide where to put each experience.

b   Write the numbers 1–6 on six small pieces of paper.

6 **Play the game.**

a   Each player in turn begins at START, chooses a piece of paper and moves the number of squares it shows. If you land on a blue square, climb the stairs. If you land on a pink square, fall down the rocky path.

b   The winner is the first player who arrives at SUCCESS.

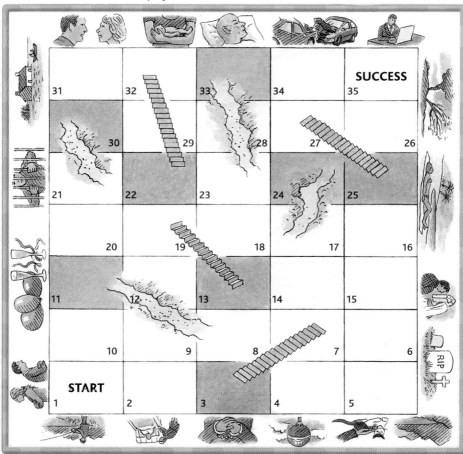